THE BACK HO

SERIES TITLES

Lessons in Geography
Phillip Sterling

Points of Tangency: Essays
Scott Russell Morris

This Season, The Next
Casey Knott

Wildlifer
Neil F. Payne

We Come from Good Stock
Kay Oakes Oring

Squatter
Yolanda DeLoach

The Arc of the Escarpment
Robert Root

Soul of the Outdoors
Dave Greschner

From the Heart: The Story of Matrix
John Harmon

The Long Fields
Anne-Marie Oomen

Kick Out the Bottom
Erik Mortenson & Christopher Kramer

Wrong Tree: Adventures in Wildlife Biology
Jeff Wilson

At the Lake
Jim Landwehr

Body Talk
Takwa Gordon

The In-Between State
Martha Lundin

North Freedom
Carolyn Dallmann

Ohio Apertures
Robert Miltner

PRAISE FOR

Lessons in Geography

"Phillip Sterling was born in the metro Detroit area and raised largely in rural West Michigan. Like earlier Michigan poets/essayists such as Theodore Roethke and Jim Harrison, Sterling, in these lovely essays, explores both the external and interior dichotomies of settled/unsettled and domestic/wild. And like his predecessors, Sterling manages to convey genuine, moving sentiment without becoming sentimental. This is a book about a poet's sometimes perilous coming of age, and of aging with grace and acceptance."

—SUE WILLIAM SILVERMAN
author of *Acetylene Torch Songs: Writing True Stories to Ignite the Soul*

"Whether writing of his northern Michigan boyhood, ancient trees, Mom's custard pie, dog bites, Belgian frites (French fries), or the abandoned death camps of Poland, Sterling brings wide-ranging insight, an in-depth sense of history, self-effacing wisdom, and the marvelous double vision of the true memoirist to these essays. His "lessons" build chronologically to depict the development of a writer's imagination with the deftness that marks his signature poetry, both complex and captivating. This fine work is a significant contribution to the Great Lakes 'Voice.'"

—ANNE-MARIE OOMEN
author of *The Long Fields*
recipient of the 2023-24 Michigan Author Award

"Phillip Sterling is one of Michigan's finest and best known poets and fiction writers. In this new collection, he raises the non-fiction bar to a new level. These wonderfully crafted essays are rich with language, alive with memory, and moving with the experiences of a rural everyday Michigan life. I highly recommend this book. *Lessons in Geography* is one of the most engaging and accessible memoirs I've read in recent years, a beautifully written narrative about place and the poetry it inspires."

—M. L. LIEBLER
author of *I Want to Be Once*
Michigan Humanities Champion of the Year, 2021

"In *Lessons in Geography,* Phillip Sterling distills a lifetime of lessons learned in places as varied as an 'Up North' Michigan lakeside cottage, a Kentucky college mailroom (where a mysterious sketch and message on a paper bag affirm his identity as a poet), and Liege, Belgium, where he explores the nuances of 'mutual understanding' in light of Belgian kissing customs. Whether describing the 'roguish' appeal of black licorice or dissecting a recipe for stollen, ingredient by memory-laden ingredient, Sterling mixes keenly observed experiences with fresh perspectives, all rendered with a poet's sensitive precision. The result is a memoir that transcends mere recollection."

—NAN SANDERS POKERWINSKI
author of *Mango Rash: Coming of Age in the Land of Frangipani and Fanta*

Lessons in Geography

The Education of a Michigan Poet

Phillip Sterling

CORNERSTONE PRESS
UNIVERSITY OF WISCONSIN-STEVENS POINT

Cornerstone Press, Stevens Point, Wisconsin 54481

www.uwsp.edu/cornerstone

Printed in the United States of America by
Point Print and Design Studio, Stevens Point, Wisconsin

Library of Congress Control Number: 2024940422
ISBN: 978-1-960329-51-6

Cornerstone Press titles are produced in courses and internships offered by the Department of English at the University of Wisconsin–Stevens Point.

To my family, literal and lyric.

In memory of my mother and father (as will be evident).

ALSO BY PHILLIP STERLING:

FICTION

Amateur Husbandry

In Which Brief Stories Are Told

POETRY

Local Congregation: Poems Uncollected 1985-2015

Short on Days

And Then Snow

And for All This: Poems from Isle Royale (chapbook)

Abeyance (chapbook)

Quatrains (chapbook)

Significant Others (chapbook)

Mutual Shores

EDITED COLLECTIONS

Imported Breads: Literature of Cultural Exchange

Isle Royale from the AIR: Poems, Stories, and Songs from 25 Years of Artists-in-Residence

CONTENTS

IV.

V.

A survey of eighteen countries found that children who play around rivers, lakes, and seas have better mental health as adults.

—"Findings," *Harper's Magazine*, January 2023

PROLOGUE: TESTING THE WATERS

It begins with bird song. At first it's a tentative coo-ah, coo-coo-coo *of a mourning dove, as though a child is blowing across the mouth of an empty Faygo bottle. Then comes the piano ping of the woodpecker, followed by the oriole's flute. Then all at once it's an orchestration of birds—warbles and chirps, house sparrow and finch, cello and violin. I may even be able to pick out the occasional reed-squawk of a red-wing or the cheer-up, cheer-up of a robin. Soon, what began as a simple sunrise solo becomes a cacophony of bird song, though less like a symphonic concert at Interlochen Music Camp's amphitheater than like the noise of a community band tuning up in the gazebo of the local park.*

In anticipation of summer's bright inactivity, I lie in bed longer than I should, pregnant with pleasure. I drift in a boat of semi-consciousness, letting my ears become accustomed to the morning. Perhaps I'll turn, ever so slightly, and expose my pinch of sunburn to the cool breeze that flutters across my bare shoulders, bringing through the patched window screen smells of cedar hedges or lilacs, or—if it had rained in the night—of worms and leaf rot and dirt. (At other times: the faint, throat-tangy sweetness of DDT or other insecticides . . . not totally unpleasant.) Contented, I'd plan no more than to lie there half asleep, beneath a loose bed sheet, free of any obligation to the day.

But if the wind comes in off the water and smells of seaweed and gasoline, I'll launch out of bed like a fireman. Dad might be just offshore in the rowboat, casting among the reeds for bass. Or maybe standing on the dock with a fly-rod and popping bug, fishing for what he liked to call "cat food." On those mornings I wouldn't want to stay in bed too long, not with crayfish to catch and seagulls to chase from the raft. I'd snatch my driest swimsuit from the clothesline—knocking off any mayflies that happened to have spent the night there—and jerk it on, shuddering at its damp and clammy cling. If I feel bold enough, or if my brothers taunt me, I'll take a quick dip in the lake before breakfast.

In the kitchen, my mother has been up for hours, boiling wild-strawberry jam or baking caramel-cinnamon coffee cake. She's always got something on the stove or in the oven, early, "before it gets too hot." If not pies and rolls, she'll be boiling eggs for deviling or potatoes for salad, or melting marshmallows for Rice Krispie treats. The kitchen will steam with promise: barbecues and picnics, treehouse lunches, fingers stained with Jell-O. Even my cold cereal—with a dollop of whipped cream or applesauce—tastes extraordinary on a morning like this . . .

IN THE EARLY 1960S, after years of weekend fishing trips and summer vacations spent in Benzie County, Michigan, where my mother's family cottage was located, my father abandoned what he called "the blood-boiling commute" down Woodward Avenue—from our house in suburban Bloomfield Hills to the Sterling Structural Steel Company in downtown Detroit—and relocated the family permanently to the more rural and easygoing region of the state, a region commonly referred to by the metropolitan Detroit tourist industry as "Up North." In our particular case, that meant we moved to what was geographically recognized as Northwest Lower Michigan. More precisely: the counties that make up the little and ring fingers of Michigan's mitt.

When I say "permanently," I'm speaking in relative terms. We moved fairly often during my formative years, though it was seldom for any length of time beyond the somewhat ill-defined boundaries of the Grand Traverse region. And once my father decided to move north, it was frequently into a house "on the water." A map of push-pins identifying our various residences would astonish most lakefront developers: Platte Lake (initially, a quarter-mile from Grandmother Urquhart's cottage), then Lake Leelanau, West Grand Traverse Bay, Lake Ann, Tibbets Lake, and so on. The rare domicile my father owned that wasn't actually waterfront—like the Bertha Vos house in Acme—was nonetheless within walking distance of a beach.

My father's initial attraction to the Grand Traverse region was not simply that it was half a day's drive (at the time) from the metropolitan area he had come to find increasingly congested and "unhealthy"; it was also one of his favorite getaways. An avid trout fisherman, Dad was particularly enamored with the Platte River, which in those days offered some of the best fly-fishing in the state. He and his high school buddy ("Mr. Blackmore") had annual reservations at Riverside, a tourist-cabined fishing camp clustered beside a deep-pooled bend on the Platte River east of Honor. My brothers and I, in fact, spent more than a few nights sleeping in one of Riverside's cramped, cigar-smoke-and-wormy-smelling cabins—at those times when more grandkids were staying at the Urquhart cottage on Big Platte Lake than our Grandmother Urquhart could tolerate. The cottage itself was partial incentive for our family's relocation Up North, as my mother—having spent innumerable summers during her adolescence and young adulthood "at the shore" (as she called it)—harbored a deep, passionate fondness for the lake through which the Platte River flowed (and shared its name).

Yet whatever possessed my father to move us repeatedly from one waterfront house to another, he never really said. Later in life—after my five siblings and I had emigrated to college or marriage or the military—he often quipped that it was simply due to the belabored chore of boxing up a household of acquisitions, hauling them to another location, and unpacking them. A chore he detested. Frequent moves (he argued, ironically) would prevent my parents from acquiring too many possessions, as each move became another opportunity to "clean house." Lakefront properties especially—often nothing more than winterized cottages—were not known for having much room for storage. Few places had anything more than a musty crawl space beneath the porch or a close, spidery, uninsulated attic where life preservers and oars would keep company in the off-season with webbed, aluminum lawn chairs. Consequently, each move necessitated donating excessive furniture and household goods to the Presbyterian Church's 'White Elephant Sale' or else passing it like family heirlooms to one of my much older siblings, who were at the time beginning to furnish houses of their own.

While more than one of my acquaintances over the years opined that the moves were probably calculated real estate investments (a fair suspicion actually, considering the feverish demand for—and consequent development of—waterfront properties during those years), it was a suspicion I scoffed at, given that many of the moves my father made were marketably lateral or even downgrades. Perhaps it was sheer restlessness on his part; or perhaps it was some dissatisfaction on my mother's. Many of their household purchases at the time were practical (read: affordable) and therefore seemed to fall short of my mother's "at the shore" aesthetics, which had been tempered by both the assumed prosperity of her family status—ownership of a summer home on the lake, for goodness' sake—and the post-war mantra of "you deserve more." Or perhaps my father was just "testing the waters," in the punning sense of exploring each locale before making a permanent commitment.

For whatever reason, my father's decision to move us Up North was instrumental in the formulation of my sense of self and perception of the world. For years I had assumed—as I imagine many of my 1968 classmates at Traverse City High School had—that the actual center of the universe was located somewhere between Point Betsie and Kalkaska, south of Beaver Island and north of Mesick.

Not until my late-blooming college ambitions landed me in Nebraska—a sixteen-hour drive from Traverse City's Clinch Park Zoo (where, during the summer after graduation from TCHS, I operated the kiddie rides, including the infamous train)—did I begin to understand how fortunate I was that so much of my childhood had such remarkable playgrounds. It took no more than a couple weeks of exploring the deliberate landscape of Hastings' ornamental shrubbery and stately trees—the latter a mere arborous blip on Nebraska's flatline of corn—before realizing how much my life would forever be tempered by my father's decision. Not everyone, I soon learned, went water-skiing after school (or even before); not everyone was only a short drive from Sleeping Bear Dunes, a sandbox the size of Washington D.C.; not everyone could ice skate in their "front yard" or drag the toboggan across the road and bobsled the old logging trails of second-growth forest; not everyone could forage his own property for fresh mushrooms, leeks, or wild strawberries.

The realization was transformative, and not just at the time, but every year since. It usually takes place when the Airbus of the school year—after a tedious and consuming nine-month flight—throttles back its jets in preparation for landing, the ETA broadcast along secondary roads in forsythia, dogwood, and morels. That's when I become antsy with anticipation. Summer beguiles me; she infuses me with memory and longing. She sidles up in her lovely humid idleness, and I am suddenly returned to mornings at the lake.

It begins with bird song . . .

Looking back over the six decades since, I wonder now if my father's restlessness was more calculated than it appears. Perhaps his moving Up North had less to do with his desires—or my mother's—than with the impact his "testing the waters" might have on his offspring. Perhaps as a native Michigander he knew that living with easy access to the boreal lakes and streams and woods and dunes of rural Michigan would fill a boy's brain with sand and marl and infuse his blood with tree sap, his spirit with poetry. That "heaven on earth" exists in more than some metaphysical sense, and that a boy, exposed to it, might well learn from it. Perhaps my father had sensed where the actual center of the universe could be found and was zeroing in on it, the way a dog circles the middle of her doggy bed before settling into sleep. Whatever the reason, there's something about my having grown up in Northern

Michigan—testing the waters, if you will—that continues to reanimate me in ways that my cultured, academic life in foreign cities or suburbia, or even in small college towns like Big Rapids, never have.

I can be anywhere—on the back deck overlooking the yard, in a classroom or faculty office of one university or another, at a hotel in Nashville or Miami or Philadelphia, even in Lublin, Poland—and when I think of summer I think of mornings on the lake. Then yesterday's disappointments burn off like an early fog, and the day ripens into possibility.

• FEB 62

I.

They were wonderful, bittersweet years.
The years I first learned about love.

MY MOTHER'S CANOE MONEY

Two or three Christmases after slot-car racing sets were in demand—at a time when most of the sixth-grade boys at Honor Elementary had either broken theirs or lost interest or else expanded the number of black and silver plastic road-pieces and bridges to a size that threatened the good nature of their parents—my brothers and I finally received ours, an inexpensive Tyco set, from Santa Claus. Our track formed a simple figure-eight, no more than four feet from outside curve to outside curve, and I remember that the metal tabs on the undercarriage of the cars bent so easily that we often had to fiddle with them in order to get the cars to run properly. I'm not sure that either of the two cars that came with the set ever worked well at the same time, but I am sure that neither of the cars worked as well as we had been led to believe they would.

The gift was no surprise, really. As an eleven-year-old, I had known for some time that "Santa Claus" was the same person who would pay my father's income tax four months after Christmas. Not to mention that a slot-car set was the only request common to my closest siblings' separate wish-lists. Nonetheless, my brothers and I were thrilled with our new toy. We *finally* belonged to that ill-defined group of "everyone else" that we had been lobbying our parents with for months. And although for the week between Christmas and New Year's we may have bickered constantly about who was going to get to run the yellow car on the inside track, we each also realized the inherent values of such a gift—a gift we had *really* wanted and that we *promised* to share with *both* our brothers—that is, the values of economy and privilege.

We were spoiled, though I wouldn't have admitted so (or even understood it) at the time. We boys seldom went without the things we *really* wanted, even despite the frustration of not getting what we wanted when we wanted them most. Often we had to wait until the popularity had worn off and the price was right. Yet in our nearsighted and obsessive concentration on the one or two things we *most* wanted, and knew we'd get, we were blind to other possibilities. We were spoiled because we didn't know what we were missing.

I didn't have a bicycle of my own until I was nine. But it never occurred to me that anyone else was any different. As the fifth of six children, I was quite often on the receiving end of well-used secondhands, especially when it came to toys. The bicycle I learned to ride on had been my grandmother's—a third-generation, chain-driven women's frame with twenty-seven or twenty-eight inch tires and a wide, unpadded seat that, by its shape and size, could have served as a home base for the community Little League team. What the original color of the bike had been I don't know; by the time my brothers and I shared it, everything but the fenders—the frame, tires, spokes, seat—had been spray-painted blue. The fenders themselves were long gone; the chrome handles of the handlebars had been sweat-worn to rust. The bike was ghastly to look at—but it was a bike nonetheless.

Old as it was, it was demonstrably bigger than the average Schwinn or Huffy that my schoolmates rode. Even with the seat lowered as far as it could go and me barely perched on it, I had difficulty keeping both feet on the pedals as I was propelled down the slight incline of our yard. Because the bike had no coaster brakes—no brakes to speak of—it could be ridden either forward or backward if a person were clever enough, and, once I mastered basic riding, I tried both ways. Needless to say, I suffered a good number of bruises and scrapes learning to ride that bike, not to mention a certain amount of embarrassment and humiliation as I maneuvered the beast through the neighborhood. Nor could I claim it as my own; I often had to take turns with whatever brother was in a snit because the other brother refused to let him run the yellow car on the inside track.

It was a bike nonetheless. I mean, we hadn't had to go without.

So when I finally got my own bike—a spiffy red, twenty-six inch Huffy—I was thrilled, pumped with the adrenaline of appreciation.

Only years later, after I had gone off to college and learned through the educational process of dorm living what my more affluent classmates' childhoods had been like, did I realize what I had gone without. Apparently, I had been led to believe through my formative years that my family was economically far better off than what we actually were. I believed we were *very* well-off, even affluent. We lived on a lake, for one thing. For another, my father for a time "collected" classic cars, including a 1932 Packard Touring. We were the first family in our neighborhood to own a color TV—years ahead of the

Joneses (not to mention years before color programming became a weekly standard of the three major networks). It wasn't until college that I realized our affluence had all been a ruse. In a kind of desire-meets-gratification bait-and-switch, my middle-class parents had continually tricked me into believing that we were financially better situated than we actually were. And they fostered my belief with canoe money.

For about the first seven or eight years of my life, my mother owned an old green wood-and-canvas canoe. Why it was my *mother's* canoe when most everything else was referred to as *ours* (excluding the classic cars, of course), I don't know. The canoe may have been given to her by one of her relatives. Or perhaps it had been included with the purchase of a house on Pine Lake in Bloomfield Hills—like the dock and the raft—which my parents bought when I was eighteen months old and my mother pregnant with my younger brother, her sixth child, having run out of space, bedroom-wise, in the small brick house they'd built in Birmingham ("For $5000," my father often boasted). Perhaps in their move to lakefront property, my mother acquired the canoe through some sort of matrimonial law of watercraft possession—the aluminum fishing boat deeded to Dad. Whatever the case, the canoe was decidedly hers.

It was longer than most canoes, and heavy, and the wooden ribs would embed flakes of varnish in our knees when we knelt on them or into our calves when we sat cross-legged in the bottom. If there were seats at all in the canoe, they'd have been wicker or woven cane and probably broken in places. We didn't have two paddles that matched.

I don't recall my mother ever using it. I can vaguely recall my older sister Judy taking us younger boys for short rides on Pine Lake, especially at dusk when the water was calm. I can remember the distinct chill-thrill of coming back into shore by cutting through the upside-down reflection of the trees, my hand dangling over the gunwale. But what I remember most about the canoe is its legacy; my mother sold it for $26 late in the 1950s.

That was, of course, years before the ubiquity of credit cards—decades before Visa or MasterCard. My father may have had a gas card or two in his wallet—he was the breadwinner then—but even as late as 1960, I can recall my mother filling her Mercury station wagon at the Shell Station in Northville (where they uniformly checked the oil and washed the windshield as well) and simply asking that the charge be "put on the tab." Most transactions were still made with cash.

Because the canoe had been my mother's, the money she received at the sale became her "canoe money"—a special fund she reserved for special purchases, like emergencies and frills. She told us—repeatedly, often at the mercy of our begging—that she kept the money in a separate compartment in her purse and that it was to be used only with the utmost discretion. Yet whenever my mother saw something for the house that she wanted (but knew we really couldn't afford)—a cat-shaped cookie jar, for instance—she'd use her canoe money. Or when she ran across a sale on a pair of pants or shoes that one of us kids could use, she'd buy them with her canoe money. Or when our birthdays came and we had been waiting months for that special present that we couldn't go without—it didn't matter that taxes were also due—Mom had "canoe money." I'm sure her canoe money bought our race car set and my first bike. Her canoe money probably bought our second color TV. Her canoe money helped pay for my college tuition. Over three decades, my mother spent her canoe money innumerable times. It became a running joke with our family.

In spite of us often teasing my mother about her phantom fund, we never hesitated to use it. It became a sort of 'cookie jar' account. Because it was a specific figure—$26—we knew it wasn't unlimited, and so we were forced to make hard decisions or choices when we wanted to spend it. At the same time, we knew we'd never have to go without anything we really, really wanted because the canoe money was always there. Where *there* was, exactly, I'm still not sure. More than once I rifled through my mother's purse—multiple purses—in search of the mysterious "separate compartment." Never found it. And not once did I suspect the whole business was my parents' way of assimilating themselves to the burgeoning credit culture. Nor, to be honest, did I care. Even if the canoe money was simply my mother's way of making do and yet giving the impression of independent wealth—*her* wealth—we were no less spoiled by it.

We were spoiled into thinking that all was well when it wasn't. We were spoiled into not worrying about money. Having the canoe money meant things would always work out all right, even if the plumbing broke or the septic tank caved in or we were eating leftover macaroni and cheese for the third dinner in a row. We always knew that we could go out to eat next week or the week after or the week after that—if we were patient. Oh, we weren't *rich* by any means. But we were secure in knowing that my mother always had a little canoe money tucked away.

THE RELISH OF SUMMER

In 1961, my father tempted both fate and fortune by selling the troubled Detroit steel company he'd taken over at my grandfather's death and investing the proceeds in one of only two year-round dining establishments in Beulah, Michigan. While it must have seemed a shrewd business move at the time—after all, Benzie County was beginning to infest with tourists in the 1960s, and *surely* the locals must have wanted go out to eat *somewhere*—he would later in his life acknowledge his naïveté as both entrepreneur and chef. The restaurant failed within two years.

They were difficult years for my parents. With my eldest brother in the Army and my eldest sister off to college, they sold the rambling five-bedroom, three-and-a-half bath lakefront house in Bloomfield Hills and downsized to a somewhat smaller ranch house in a new subdivision further out in the suburbs (Northville) and a two-bedroom (and sleeping porch), one-bath cottage on Platte Lake, a short distance from my grandmother's. My parents had planned, I imagine, to simply spend their summers—as well as the occasional weekend or holiday—Up North, much in the way my mother had during her formative years. And for a year or so, that's what we did, nomadically, with the lengths of time we spent at the cottage on

Platte Lake seeming to increase with every visit. When the restaurant opportunity in Beulah enticed my father into a career change—and "permanent" relocation to a region of the state most of the family had come to prefer—we moved lock-stock-and-barrel into the cottage.

The accommodations were cramped, to say the least, as there were still four of us six children living at home. And the seasonal, rustic nature of wicker or aluminum furnishings took some getting used to, especially for those members of the family who'd grown accustomed to davenports, overstuffed armchairs, and ottomans. (Not to mention TV.) Winterization of our Platte Lake 'house,' for instance, consisted of 4 mil plastic tacked over the screens and the retrofit installation of a propane space heater.

My father—and any child big enough to help—spent long hours at the restaurant; my mother (with an uncanny prescience of impending failure) had already re-matriculated at MSU in hopes of finishing the teaching degree she'd abandoned years before. She spent a good deal of time commuting to East Lansing.

But for me—a ten-year-old boy with a Huffy bike and a BB gun, and hills upon hills of undeveloped woodland as a backyard, and Platte Lake in the front, not to mention two rowboats at my disposal, one with a 10-horse Johnson outboard—they were glorious years. They were years of innocence and experience; years when a shy, imaginative boy, left to his own resources, could ride roughshod over abandonment and delinquency. Years of piracies and poison ivy, of mosquitoes and hide-and-seek, of renegade baseball games and fingers the color of whatever Jell-O I'd stolen from the cupboard. Of Fizzies and phosphates. Of crayfish teased from clamshells, and fishing with hot dogs off the dock.

Oh, I had bad times during those years, to be sure, but they had little to do with economic responsibility, or even comfort. Instead, my only real difficulties were with pangs of adolescence. In looking back now, the physical injuries I suffered were mostly tempered by amusements; my losses I've come to accept as lessons well learned.

They were wonderful, bittersweet years. The years I first learned about love.

I had two loves at the time. One was my cousin Nancy. Born just weeks before I was, she was enough like me in looks and behavior that we'd often be mistaken for twins. During summer vacation, when Nancy and her sisters overran my grandmother Urquhart's cottage, we were inseparable. From the moment Mr. Bixler, next door, rang his farm bell—which he did, every day at 8 a.m.—until we'd been called for the umpteenth time to "Come in and get ready for bed," Nancy and I were together. Exploring. Fishing. Swimming. Even during the requisite rest-hour after lunch, when we couldn't go swimming ("You'll get cramps"), Nancy and I would sit together on the porch, reading Hardy Boys or Nancy Drew, or playing Chinese checkers. On high-starred nights, when my brothers and cousins and any kids staying in the rentals down the way played hide-and-seek in Bixler's evergreen field, if Nancy was *it*, I would be the first to give myself away, giggling or jittering in the cedars so she'd find me.

Nancy was more than simply my best friend; I was *attracted* to her, as were many of the boys our age (or slightly older) who summered on Platte Lake. As the youngest of my Aunt Sue's three girls—popular, good-looking, free-spirited "teens"—Nancy was adventurous and playful, confident and reckless, mature, even *sexy* (though only in retrospect would I apply such a term—after all, it was the *early* '60s and, at ten years old, I'd likely seldom heard the word spoken). My love for her was no doubt in part due to her freshness and maturity, especially when it came to issues of boy-girl intimacy. She was the first girl to pay any attention to me, and it wasn't until much later that I came to understand how much of her companionship was due to familial proximity and common interests than out of any real infatuation.

My other love was pickles. *Dill* pickles, to be precise. And I'm not talking about the bullfrog-colored, kosher deli types that are ubiquitous in rural Michigan bars—often found beside fleshy jugs of pickled bologna—nor those sealed individually in plastic pouches and stacked like green summer sausages in the dairy coolers of IGAs. I'm talking about the premier of sour, caustic relishes: *hamburger dill slices.* The kind of pickle that most people would cautiously add as a garnish to a barbequed ground chuck patty, for they are notoriously vinegary: dill slices will cause one's eyes to squint and weep and one's cheeks to pucker into unsightly contortions. (Even now, as I write this, with the closest hamburger dill slices at Family Fare, two miles away, just the thought of them makes my salivary glands hose down the riot of my taste buds . . .)

I loved pickles almost as much as I loved Nancy. And I loved Nancy in part because she loved pickles as much as I did.

My father, as the proprietor of a small-town restaurant, would buy pickles in three-gallon jugs. He'd purchase them wholesale from Gordon Food Service, as he did the equally impressive aquariums of mayonnaise or ketchup. But my cousin Nancy and I—notorious "sourpusses"—weren't allowed to snitch too many from the restaurant, since my father was afraid we'd eat the whole twelve quarts and make ourselves sick. (Or worse yet: that there wouldn't be any left to garnish his famed grilled cheese sandwiches, a popular lunch special . . .) Instead, my mother would purchase thirty-two-ounce jars of Ann Page Dill Slices from the A&P, and Nancy and I would be allowed to snack to our stomachs' marvelous content, often finishing the jar in a few days.

We loved dill pickles, Nancy and I. At holiday gatherings or Sunday dinners, we'd empty the pickles from the relish tray as soon as my mother set it on the folding table that served as our formal buffet, leaving only celery sticks and black olives. Or, better yet, we'd volunteer to prepare the tray and by doing so get to eat as many pickles as we wanted to *before* dinner. (More often, we'd be chased out of the kitchen at first snatch, ordered to "Stay out of the pickles!" and "Don't spoil your appetite!")

I recall once removing from the Frigidaire a nearly full jar of hamburger dill slices to sustain us as Nancy and I moseyed the familiar quarter mile from our house to my grandmother's cottage. By the time we'd stopped at Fisher Creek to jig for frogs, only the greenish juice, spotted with soft, pale seeds, was left. We emptied it into the creek—after all, it was about the same color—and then used the jar to capture minnows.

We were pickle enthusiasts. Pickle gourmands. Pickle freaks. "Pickle pusses." At every chance, we tried new recipes: pickles on peanut butter sandwiches; pickles on grilled cheese, with bacon; pickles sandwiched between potato chips; pickles in place of a Hershey's candy bar on s'mores (not recommended); even pickles and ice cream (not so bad on vanilla; not so good on spumoni). Once we'd blended them with grape Kool-Aid and ice milk, a kind of pickle frappé . . . (also not recommended).

How much of our extraordinary taste for pickles was actually due to a culinary preference for cucumbers saturated with vinegar and garlic, and how much was mere adolescent attention-getting, I can no longer say. But to this day I maintain a peculiar fondness for dill pickles—of any kind—and the single bite of a Claussen or Vlasic will transport me back to one of the happiest periods of my life.

Alas! Neither summer nor adolescence lasts. Nancy blossomed into a full-fledged teenager over the next few years—forging junior high and high school friendships in Plymouth, where my aunt and uncle "wintered"—while I spent more time by myself, often doing solo what she and I would have done together. I tried to keep her close in that way. But on the day I was jigging for frogs in Fisher Creek and by accident whipped a hornets' nest with my bamboo pole, I had what James Joyce called an "epiphany." I ran wildly back home, leaving Bixler Road strewn with certain buzzing articles of my clothing, and as I sat gasping, sweaty and tearful, while my mother tried to salve all the stings, I reluctantly accepted the fact that I would never be able to marry my first cousin, no matter how I felt about her, and that love, from that point on, for all its attraction, would always be a little sour.

GIVIN' SUMMER THE BUSINESS

On a recent visit to Lake Michigan, Andrew—the youngest of our four children—was the first to come running back from a beachcombing expedition.

"Dad, look!" he shouted, thrusting under my nose a 16-ounce plastic cup filled with assorted shore wash: clam shells, snail shells, barnacle-like shells, and shells of assorted other indistinguishable mollusks or crustaceans. Judging by the cup's proximity to my face, he was obviously proud of his collection.

"Great!" I said, careful to sound enthusiastic. Only days before I had recycled a few thousand such shells, as well as multicolored pebbles, seagull feathers, water glass, and fragments of driftwood that Andrew's brother and sisters had scavenged and carted home from previous visits to the beach, not to mention hundreds of similar souvenirs in the sandwich bags and plastic buckets brought back from visits to Connecticut, Maine, Vermont, North Carolina, and elsewhere. The rock garden behind our house was fast becoming some future geo-archaeologist's nightmare.

I feigned a fatherly interest. "So what do you plan to do with them?"

"Sell them," he said, matter-of-factly. "SHELL CITY!" The conviction in his voice mimicked a local car dealer's TV ad.

"Sounds good," I replied, hoping the tone of my voice registered confidence, despite my certain knowledge that Shell City would likely go the way of most youthful entrepreneurships—down the tubes. Even without a recession, the odds of Shell City franchises supporting the tourist industry of various coastal regions were, at best, long shots. While Andrew would no doubt gain something from the venture—learn some hard lessons about free enterprise and proprietorship—not to mention hard work—I suspected that eventually his enthusiasm would founder and the whole business be abandoned to the ocean of capitalism.

My suspicion was based on experience.

When I was about Andrew's age, my brothers and I concocted an assortment of summer ventures (*ad*-ventures, actually) in an attempt to make our early fortunes, which in those days we had calculated to be at least three dollars—one dollar a piece. Unaware of even the most elemental principles of supply and demand, or capital gains (and losses), we had acted solely in response to two basic economic indicators: (1) my brother Richard's prior success, and (2) summer's stifling doldrums.

My brother Richard was our mentor, our Howard Hughes. He was living proof that wealth meant nothing more than being in the right place at the right time. A mostly shy, somewhat quiet child, he nevertheless found innumerable opportunities to regale us of the day he just happened to be out on Pine Lake in our 14-foot aluminum boat when he saw a fisherman stranded by an uncooperative outboard motor. No sooner had Richard towed the old guy into shore behind our 10-horse Johnson than he was rewarded with a five-dollar bill. In those days of penny licorice, five dollars was a lot of candy. And so easy!

The next day Richard painted "Dickie Bird's Towing Services" on both sides of the aluminum bow with gold model-airplane paint. He spent the better part of the week cruising the shoreline for customers. I don't recall now whether his advertising ever paid off, but I can still see him waving the five simoleons in front of our faces and bragging like an investment broker in a bull market. There was certainly more where that came from. So by the time we moved later that year, and sold Richard's towing business with the Bloomfield Hills house, my brothers and I had been impaled on the American Dream. Its barbs were embedded.

For the next few years, our home was more often than not a winterized cottage on Platte Lake. Located on a dirt-packed one-lane road well off the paved highway, the cottage was isolated in a part of the state that had yet to be discovered by very many tourists; it would be years before Senator Hart pushed for National Lakeshore status of our "local" dunes. Not a particularly good location for the traditional lemonade or Kool-Aid stand, it was nevertheless beside that rural, off-the-beaten path that my brothers and I established business after business, the cool phosphate of Richard's five dollars still on our tongues.

We first thought we could pave the road to wealth with Petoskey stones. Indigenous to both nearby Lake Michigan and Platte Lake (but rare in other parts of the state—or so we had been told), we had noticed that their polished and mounted counterparts drew much attention—and commanded cold cash—in local souvenir stores and tourist shops. Although we ourselves failed to find any stones water-honed in mitten shapes or in the likenesses of bears—as I'm sure we assumed we would—Platte Lake provided an easy abundance of Petoskey stones without much effort on our parts.

After one brief morning of collection, we had a card table full of various sizes—from smaller than a magic bean to bigger than a basketball. We figured that unsuspecting passersby would pay scads of money for Petoskey stones, and unaware of anything like clarity or quality, we priced them according to size. No doubt influenced by automakers' claims of "Bigger is Better," we tagged the little ones a nickel apiece, and for the ones we couldn't even lift to the table (and which, admittedly, may have had only a patch or vein of fossil) we were asking two dollars. We calculated that half a dozen big ones would set us up for life.

But marketing was a problem. We soon realized that if we expected to have traffic jams in our parking area then we had to get people to drive down our road. So we unearthed a few scraps of wood Dad had hidden behind the garage, painted them, and nailed the signs to the trees out by the highway. I think it was my idea to abbreviate, given the size of our wood scraps: 'TOSKY STONZ. Then we set up chairs and waited for Opportunity to pull its black Cadillac into the yard. We expected by noon to be able to buy that keen battery-powered motorboat in the Beulah Drugstore. What we hadn't figured on was how little traveled the main road actually was. We had forgotten how often we had ridden our bikes as far as the Cherry Bowl Drive-In in Honor without ever seeing a car. So after an hour or so of sitting in the sun and squabbling about how we'd split two dollars three ways—if it came to that—Richard decided we'd fare better as a self-serve. We left a coffee can on a paper plate that read "Please Leave Correct Change" and went swimming.

No one stopped all afternoon. We closed down the next day, when Mom came looking for her good card table.

We tried live bait. A man over on the Platte River sold nightcrawlers for 50 cents a dozen, so we advertised ours at 45 cents (which Richard determined could be divided three ways more easily). We'd gone out with our Cub Scout flashlights one night after a rain and snatched up the slimy investments as they lay in the wet grass. We put them in a cigar box with some dried leaves and moss. New signs went up at the paved road; we nailed a PAY HERE to the garage. Then we waited. And waited. Impatience finally drove us out of the market. We used up all our stock fishing for bluegills and sunfish under the raft.

One time we filled a metal washtub with crayfish. We had caught them by the dozens beneath the stones and clam shells along shore, including a few females, their eggs still clumped like tapioca beneath the tail. We calculated that in a few short days we'd have hundreds of tiny crayfish scooting backwards around the tub. In a week, at 25 cents apiece, instant wealth! Just add water!

That night the raccoons scattered the husks of our profit in every direction—and we hadn't been insured for loss.

So it went summer after summer. Except for Little League candy bars or Boy Scout raffle tickets—which we couldn't really count since the income went to someone else—we weren't very successful in sales. And while eventually we would learn that there were other ways to make money, we also learned that real effort was often involved.

One year I planted a garden. I had pestered my father all spring to have a local farmer disk a plot in the backyard. With vegetable and fruit stands on every crossroads between Honor and Beulah—the two closest villages to

Platte Lake—I assumed it was a sure thing. I invested in rows and rows of radishes and string beans, a handful of tomato plants, and carrots. All I could afford.

The radishes grew fat and hot that summer, though my brothers ate them as fast as they were pulled. We had green beans by the grocery sack—if you could find the plants among the weeds. No one had told me about weeds. In no time at all the weeds overpowered the carrots and tomatoes. Finally, when I took a single bag of beans to Harold's market in Honor and Harold (somewhat reluctantly) agreed to buy my complete harvest, wholesale, for 39 cents, I gave up farming.

Despite repeated failures, we never seemed to figure out that there was no such thing as easy money. The closest we ever came to making a profit was not in sales but in the service industry. When our grandmother came to visit, she'd pay handsomely for pints of wild strawberries or blackberries. But a morning's kneeling and bending over small plants among the poison ivy along the road—or fighting the prickers in hot sun—convinced me that my fortune wasn't in picking fruit. It was too much work for a so-called summer "vacation."

Ever since those adolescent attempts (except for a brief and unsuccessful foray into marketing as a partner in a specialized greeting card company—when I spent the better part of July unsuccessfully peddling eight Christmas designs), I've tried to avoid the entire sales experience. At the same time, I can appreciate the lessons that most small businessmen will learn, often the hard way. If I could, I would explain those lessons to Andrew ahead of time so he could avoid the frustration and anxiety of that misnomer: "free" enterprise.

On the other hand, if Andrew does choose to set up Shell City in the backyard and proffers Lake Michigan backwash to unsuspecting urban folks (who could find the same shells by the quadrillions at any public beach), I won't be the one to discourage him. If anything, as a supportive father and believer in fair business practices, I'd probably invest in a few choice beauties myself.

THE LICORICE OF POLITICS

"The torch has been passed to a new generation of Americans."

—John F. Kennedy, 1960

I had little concern for politics in 1960. While I celebrated my tenth birthday the week after John F. Kennedy's narrow election was confirmed, it was a time when few adults expected someone my age to comprehend the magnitude of what was already taking place in Cuba by the time General Eisenhower turned over the throttle of government to the young PT 109 commander. But that's not to suggest I was completely oblivious to the cold front of bureaucratic change. Surely something other than wind tussled Robert Frost as he recited "The Gift Outright" at Kennedy's inauguration—something like electricity, a charge of promise and power—like *atomic* power—which, when harnessed for its beneficial properties, would surely help lift into space the Conestoga wagon of the New Frontier.

Even as a ten-year-old, I sensed something in the blustery, celebratory air of Robert Frost's gifting—a chilly apprehension, a fear that the future was known only to itself and that in the absence of certainty was the poem of all that could go wrong. It was a kind of excitement tempered by post-war ambiguity, a feeling that I got not so much from the news items I'd pasted in my fifth grade current events folder as from my involvement in the youth choir at the First Presbyterian Church in Northville, Michigan, during the seminal months of the Nixon-Kennedy campaign.

I joined the choir early in 1960, halfway through the fourth grade. My reasons for mounting such a bus mid-journey were numerous, but they included the fact that we had moved to Northville at the beginning of the academic year, and it had taken much of the fall for my mother to formally un-tithe her commitment to Kirk in the Hills. It was nearly Advent before we were considered part of the regular congregation in Northville and so it was not until rehearsals for the Christmas Eve pageant that I felt very comfortable with the other youth in the church. By Epiphany, however, I had come to realize as I squirmed in the stiff-backed pews between my two writhing, intolerable brothers (lined up, as we often were, by order of age) that there may be benefits to sitting in front of the sanctuary—like padded chairs. Besides, if I sang in the youth choir during the first service, satisfying my mother's insistence that we "participate in church," I could then attend Sunday School with kids my age, instead of the boring, communion-lengthy second service, which was the one preferred by my late-sleeping older siblings. So when the call for additional youth choir members was sounded, I joined the robe-winged ranks of the near-angelic.

At first, I enjoyed youth choir, though not because I fancied myself a particularly good singer or even a devout Presbyterian. Prior to 1960, I'd dismissed churchgoing as something akin to politics, which had all the attraction of abstract art, like the paintings done by elephants that I'd seen on the cover of *Life* magazine. Yet the more involved I became, the more I enjoyed it, and the more I came to appreciate its subtle possibilities. For the first time, I was sharing in an activity stimulated by opportunity, if not pleasure. It made me feel good about myself; it gave me purpose. Suddenly my life—not unlike (I imagined) the lives of many Americans at the time—began to bloom with promise, and, if it all somehow paralleled the springtime surge of Kennedy's presidential campaign, so much the better.

Choir practice was held once a week after school. Because I was *nearly* ten, and Northville at the time held the small-town mystique of being a safe, quiet, conservative, suburban environment (with decent schools), I was allowed to walk by myself from the elementary school on North Center Street to the First Presbyterian Church on Main Street. A route which led me past The Sweet Shop, Woolworth's, the Rexall Drugstore, and the Cloverdale Dairy ice cream parlor. Since school got out about 3 p.m. and choir practice didn't begin until 4:30—and since my mother's guilt for not being able to transport me provided me with supplemental allowance (she was commuting to East Lansing for classes)—I was free to spend an hour or so dawdling at confectionary establishments, liberating my desires.

Occasionally I would buy chocolate. I have always loved chocolate—Nestlé's bars, M&M's, Brach's bridge mix, even the hard chunks of solid generic chocolate the saleswomen at Woolworth's would thwack off with a small hammer-like tool, weigh on silver-bowled confectioner's scales, and tilt into small white bags. I love the rich, sweet, oily way chocolate lingers in my mouth, the velvety coating it leaves in the back of my throat. (To this day, I find it difficult to pass through check-outs at Walmart or Meijer without hustling a few Midnight Milky Ways onto the conveyor belt . . .) It is surely an addiction, though I'd argue that it is less one of cocoa bean chemistry and more of genetics and consumer affluence. My mother, whose sweet tooth eventually evolved into dentures, saw to it that our house was seldom without candy, of which chocolate was only one type. Yet, despite my chocophilia, during those weekly walks across the village of Northville in 1960, I was more likely to buy long thin strings of licorice—by the white paper bagful—which I'd untangle and then braid or knot into a dozen forms before I'd shove the whole wad into my mouth.

Black licorice especially. Unlike chocolate, which had proven its upscale status by appearing in etched candy dishes on my mother's coffee table—those that didn't hold spiced gumdrops or cellophane-wrapped ice-blue mints—there was something devilishly protestant about black licorice. Something un-Presbyterian. Not only did it taint my teeth with a delinquent, tobacco-like stain, it also left in my mouth a somewhat unsavory smell that I'm sure advertised to my fellow choristers what I had done. (Nor was I averse to eating a little during choir practice itself.) I was convinced there was something roguish about black licorice, something sacrilegious, in spite of—or maybe because of—its glorious and gritty taste. It was *bitter*-sweet. For a boy on the verge of adolescence, licorice was as risky as cigarettes. Still, as long as I had my own allowance and was allowed to amble through the village of Northville unescorted on my way to choir practice, I was free to buy it. And simply because I was *able to* gave me reason enough to become a regular customer at The Sweet Shop every Thursday afternoon on my way to choir. [*Oh what liberties this Great Country fosters!*]

Black licorice has a taste like nothing else. When it's fresh, the thin strings swing loosely, like overcooked spaghetti, and soften pleasantly in the mouth. Its flavor is both caramel and tangy, like a good smoked cheese. Or like an ice cream float made with Vernors ginger ale and orange sherbet. Of course, when licorice is stale, it's harsh and salty, and it leaves a nasty aftertaste, not unlike (I imagine) chewing asphalt or roofing tar. The strands break apart and lodge uncomfortably between the teeth. Half-chewed pieces gag in the throat.

And yet . . . how often does one's addiction appear more like a good friend than the playground bully? Even in spite of the numerous times that I bought black licorice which turned out rancid—for licorice in particular has a tendency toward staleness and difficulty—disappointment seldom softened my desire. The next week I'd again be found pointing through my reflection in the glass displays at the candy store to the pasta of black licorice that nestled there, a fistful of quarters in my sweaty palm.

Truth be told, my inability to recognize black licorice's tendency toward staleness stemmed in large part from trying to please Julie Cousins, the only girl who paid any attention to me at the time and my *real* reason for joining choir in the first place. Julie was one of the few people I'd ever willingly shared candy with. She honestly seemed to like me, and as I was moving toward adolescence in 1960, the year I began to discover an interest in girls, it was important that someone like Julie paid attention in return. We became friends—choir friends, licorice friends,

Sunday School friends—though I seldom spoke to her outside of church. Nor did I see her more than once or twice during the summer between fourth and fifth grades, since my family spent as much time as we could at our cottage (soon to be our house) Up North. It was a typical pre-adolescent infatuation, a one-sided adoration from afar, and I was perfectly happy with that, excited as much by the promise as by the practice. In that respect, Julie represented to me more a form of religion than of politics, and so, much like James Joyce's narrator in "Araby," I "bore my chalice safely through a throng of foes." In my naiveté, I even assumed it would last forever.

But my assumption proved false. One cool Sunday in October, when the sanctuary was filled with the fragrance of apple cider and pumpkin doughnuts—not to mention the leafy smoke of presidential campaign fires—I was not only unsettled by the power-mongering of the nascent women's movement but was jarred into political awareness as well.

It happened shortly after the first service. Upon disentangling myself from the red robe and gold collar of the youth choir's morning plumage, I went to Sunday School in the basement of the church as usual, only to find the classroom door shut and locked. At first, I suspected an innocent prank. I knew that the other kids from choir had already gone into their classrooms, and none of the kids my age were in the hall. Giggles coming from behind the closed door confirmed my suspicions. I knocked.

"Who's there?" said a rough voice, deep in intentional disguise.

"Phillip," I answered.

"What do you want?"

"I want in. Where's Mr. K.?" As our teacher was not known to put up with such shenanigans, I'd concluded that he wasn't there yet. At the same time, given the logic of adults saddled with promoting doctrine to a dozen or so sugar-fed pre-adolescents, I was afraid that when he did come, if I was the one caught in the hall, I'd be the one in trouble.

"Let me in, please," I said.

There were brief murmurings. Then a voice said, "Friend or foe?"

"Friend," I said, hopefully.

"Prove it," said a different voice. It was followed by more whispering.

"How?"

"Who do you want for president?" said Julie, the words throaty and muffled. The whispering stopped. The silence behind the door was eager for my response.

Frankly, I didn't know what to say. Up until then, I had had no real political preferences. To a boy of nearly ten, what was happening in the rest of the world seemed remote to what was happening in the cul-de-sac of Woodland Farms subdivision. Still, I knew I had to say something. I didn't want Julie—or anyone else who may have been behind the door—to think badly of me. I was, after all, on the launch pad of adolescence. So I weighed the possibilities. On the one hand, a lot of people liked John Kennedy. He was handsome and energetic; he had children nearly my age. On the other hand, I'd heard members of my family say that "Good looks don't make a good president,"—not to mention the fact that Kennedy was not only a Democrat but (Gasp!) a *Catholic*. Eisenhower, in contrast, had seemed to be a well-respected leader—the very General (for goodness sakes!) under whom my father had served in Europe—and wasn't his Vice President deemed honorable? In a staunchly Republican congregation, the odds were on status quo.

"Richard Nixon," I said.

"YUCK!" came the reply. And then—too late—it occurred to me. I was talking to a group of Gidget-worshippers, who no doubt preferred Elvis to Sinatra and would barely be able to identify the movie scores of Henry Mancini. They would vote for good looks.

I had blundered into politics.

"I mean *John Kennedy*," I said quickly. But the door didn't open. And for the next ten minutes or so, no matter how I tried to convince the unyielding partisan mob of my *true* political persuasions, I got nowhere. I begged and pleaded, I bartered licorice—all to no avail. By the time tardy Mr. K. arrived, I had not only given up on getting back into the good graces of the fifth-grade girls, but I'd also pledged myself to a lifetime of political apathy. And it was just as well. Julie seldom spoke to me after that.

WE MOVED UP NORTH THAT SUMMER, which helped soothe my recovery from the love-bashing. Yet despite the limited technological advances in electronic media at the time—we lived down the road from my grandmother's cottage on Platte Lake, in Benzie County, barely within reach of the Traverse City television broadcasts—it was difficult to keep my apolitical pledge. I felt the tension in the air during the Cuban missile crisis, for instance, even if I didn't completely understand why the voices on the radio sounded so strained, so intense. I can remember watching "the drained faces of Negro school-children rise like balloons"—as the poet Robert Lowell apparently also had—which appeared as nothing more than shadowy gray confrontations on the one TV channel we did manage to get, occasionally. I remember Khrushchev banging his shoe in the ads for U.S. Savings Bonds. But only vaguely do I recall the Berlin blockade and subsequent rise of the Iron Curtain, since at Honor Elementary School our current events consisted more of U.S. satellites and the March of Dimes.

I think I can remember my sister, a college student during the Kennedy years, talking about whether or not to join the Peace Corps. But I can't any longer be sure. The voice I hear comes from a capricious memory, which is more than likely tempered by consequence and disbelief.

I simply may have been breathing in the same smog of disappointment that the American public began to scent in the air as Kennedy's administration cranked to full production. The positive accomplishments served in the course of the first Hundred Days had had a gravy of rhetoric and rumor. So as the media played loud, quick, catchy tunes of Broadway musicals, I think most Americans suspected that the instruments were being blown with the cold breath of uncertainty as the United States jockeyed into world dominance.

Either that, or I was still reeling from Julie Cousins.

Admittedly, much of my attention was focused on more domestic affairs. The winters of '61 and '62 were the worst that our region of Michigan suffered in years, which meant they were glorious for boys who dug bomb shelters in the snow that our father piled to the height of gutters by shoveling off the roof of the garage so it wouldn't collapse. During the summers, I spent much of the time with my cousin Nancy. I learned to water ski. I camped with the Boy Scouts in the unspoiled woods of Senator Hart's future National Lakeshore. I learned how to whittle; I learned first aid. I planted a garden. By the time I entered seventh grade in Honor, I was in love again, this time with Carol and Cathy White, the twins, who I also admired from a distance because I had convinced myself that I didn't know which one I liked better. It appeared that despite the well-advertised and flamboyant threats of Castro and Khrushchev, my life would continue to roll out effortlessly ahead of me. And because of our rural location, with the closest candy store a healthy bike ride away, I lost my addiction to licorice.

WE MOVED AGAIN IN THE FALL OF 1963. My mother, upon completion of her education degree and certification, accepted a teaching job with the Traverse City Public Schools. So, on the blue threshold of my early teens, I was able to make another fresh start, at Traverse City Junior High.

Clearly, I was not unused to change. Up until then, I'd been able to adapt readily to the role of new-kid-in-school. But suddenly, I was in unfamiliar territory. Traverse City Junior High was a large, three story building—bigger than any school I had attended thus far—and it included ninth grade, which tipped socialization untenably toward teenager activities. Boys jockeyed aggressively for girls' attention. The school administration, in fact, encouraged such behavior. The small size of the cafeteria required lunch hour to be divided into thirds; we were assigned twenty minutes to eat. During the rest of the period, the vice principal would act as disc jockey and play music over the PA in the gymnasium so students who weren't eating could dance if they wanted to—to rock and roll!

Bittersweet. Perhaps it was just my age, on the cusp of "teens," the transition to adolescence. Or perhaps it was Traverse City's long history of strong school alliance and old family genealogy (given its distance from the downstate cities with comparably-sized schools) which closed to newcomers the doors of hallway friendships (or cliques). Perhaps it was a simply a kind of immaturity, my closest sibling models of "teenager" having consisted of a wallflowerish sister (already off to college) and a geeky, reclusive brother. Or perhaps it was just something in the autumn air. But whatever the reason, I felt alien, unsure of myself.

And yet . . . there was the Kennedy administration—a future smiling beyond the crowded halls of Traverse City Junior High. A taste of stability and confidence. "Youthful" confidence, it had been called. A promise of *the moon*, for goodness sake! In the glitter of handsome optimism, I could see the hints of happier days ahead. Not only that, I finally had a bedroom of my own, to which I could confine myself (if necessary) from the jousts of sibling rivalry. For my thirteenth birthday, I was given what I had asked for: a portable *stereo* phonograph, with a drop-down turntable and speakers that could be unhooked and separated to a distance of almost six feet.

By November, then, I had assimilated fairly well (I thought) to the culture of junior high. I'd made a few friends, if only due to riding the school bus together or being in the same Scout troop (friends that were obviously more knowledgeable than I about gender jostling or rock music and who were more than willing to involve me in their confidences). I'd also become quite adept at dealing with awkward social circumstances in the same way that I'd learned to garner attention at our rambunctious, family-of-eight Sunday dinners—I joked, and teased, and clowned. "A future comic," my father once remarked.

Sadly, it all came to an end in Spanish I. We were in the middle of oral recitation—muddling through our unison count to twenty ("*catorce . . . quince . . . dieciséis . . . diecisiete . . .*")—when the vice principal came to the door and asked to speak to Mrs. Cowie in the hall. She immediately charged Kathy C. (*Teacher's Pet!*) with responsibility for leading us through the numbers again, correctly, and then left the room. Kathy did her best—*uno, dos, tres*—but the lesson soon became punctuated by inattention. It was, after all, Friday, and we'd just come from lunch period, where students had been dancing to "Limbo Rock" or drumming "Wipe Out" with pencils on their books. Not to mention that the third-level classroom was stifling, unseasonably warm. Some students simply turned away from Kathy's lead; others followed reluctantly, or with undue tenor. I muffed Spanish in my best Donald Duck voice.

When Mrs. Cowie finally returned, she was physically shaken, and, to our surprise, said nothing about our childish behavior. Instead, she took a moment to compose herself and then announced that the President had been shot. As a senior faculty member and coordinator of the foreign language classes, she'd been asked to inform the other teachers. The rest of the period, she said, would be a study hall, monitored by Kathy, and that she trusted us as "mature eighth graders" to behave appropriately.

No sooner had the door closed behind Mrs. Cowie than shades of a Spanish insurrection broke out. Kathy, and one or two of the other more mature girls, began to cry. The rest of us reacted in typical junior high fashion. We laughed and threw papers. We took candy and gum out of our desks and passed it around. We wondered out loud if we'd get to go home early.

"Hey, Kathy," I shouted, over the hubbub. "How do you say 'dead-as-a-doornail' in Spanish?"

"It's *muerto*-something, isn't it?" said Bobby, the first in our class to let his hair grow over his collar, which had prompted his lawyer-father to argue the dress code policy with the School Board. "Like in *Dia de los Muertos*. Remember at Halloween, when The Cow brought in those skeleton cookies?"

"Oh yeah," I said, flipping through the barely-thumbed glossary of my Spanish book. "But what's the word for *doornail* . . ."

I was being cute, I thought, funny. I was reacting as any shy, new-kid looking for attention would act under the pressure of confusion—I masked my apprehension and fear in obnoxiousness.

So I cracked a lot of jokes over the next few days—as the President's head slumped in Jackie's lap dozens of times on TV; as Oswald was captured by Dallas police and then shot by Jack Ruby; as John, Jr., saluted his father's coffin at the funeral . . . And then it became tedious—all those images replayed and replayed, the individual frames of film, the trajectory of a bullet (or two or three), spread out in a special collector's issue of *Life* magazine. The jokes grew stale. Then not funny at all. Suddenly, the world wasn't what I thought it would be. It was small and uncomfortable; it brought misery and sadness into our living room. I began to consider how uncertain our lives really are, and how superficial. How promise can be lost in a shot.

For the rest of that school year I had an awful taste in my mouth—as though a piece of black licorice were stuck stubbornly in my teeth. I didn't any longer anticipate the joys and pleasures of childhood, as I did in Northville when I used to walk to choir. Instead, I felt slightly betrayed, like when I was locked out of the Sunday School classroom by Julie and the others.

To this day I blame President Kennedy—if not Kennedy himself, then his death, the death of all the dreams and ideals that his administration led us to believe in, as all adolescents are led by advertising and rhetoric—the moony promises of a New Frontier, a secure and comfortable place, where human beings live in prosperity and happiness. It was more than a promise of freshness, of future; we were promised a "better" future.

But it was simply the same licorice in new packaging. As it is every election year. And while there may be claims of a guarantee—the refund of my purchase price if I'm not completely satisfied—many of the companies that made those claims have closed their doors for good.

ROBERT

People are often surprised at how little I know about my eldest brother. If I mention him during a casual conversation, I am certain to be served questions that I can't volley. I know *basic* information about him, of course, but, even if pressed, I can't come up with any more personal details. I'd have to do a lot of estimating about his age, as Robert was born more than a decade before I was, and I couldn't tell you his date of birth. I'm not sure what his hobbies or interests were, or even if he had any. I know less about him than I do about some suddenly intimate acquaintances I've encountered in the Detroit Metro airport while awaiting a delayed flight.

My ignorance is embarrassing, at times; after all, he was my brother.

I was only six or seven when Robert joined the Army, immediately after his graduation from Bloomfield Hills High School. I'm not sure of the exact year, although I vaguely remember that the Kirk in the Hills Presbyterian Church had been struck by lightning about the same time—possibly the night of Robert's graduation—and my Sunday School class was temporarily moved to the high school during reconstruction, a move that caused my brother to remark that at least *he* didn't have to go there any longer. It must have been 1956 or 1957.

What visual memories I have of my brother probably can be credited more to the antics my father captured on 16-millimeter film during birthdays and holidays than to my actual recollection. In the same way that family legends we've heard a hundred times become a part of our own storytelling, we tend to conceive some of our memories second-hand, out of images that come to us later in our lives. I don't actually remember going after our RCA TV with a wooden mallet when I was a toddler, for example, but I've seen myself do it on film so many times that it's now become a scene from my autobiography, a visual—and therefore accurate— representation of my "memory." I've internalized it into a pseudo-memory.

As a result, much of what I can recall about my brother's youth—the short time we occupied the same house—is a kind of sequence of film clips: my brother clowning at his sixteenth birthday party; my brother sledding with my cousins on Christmas afternoon; my brother talking upside down on the phone; my brother in imitation leopard-skin pants running through the dining room of our house on Middlebelt; my brother getting married in his Army uniform.

Other "memories" are less vivid, more like rumors. I can recall, I think, an old Ford parked for months in the tall grass just beyond the driveway. Robert had spray-painted it gold—completely, right down to the tires and bumpers—and, the story goes, he dressed all in gold himself—pants, shirt, socks, belt, even his shoes—when he drove the car to a school dance. I believe he got up early during his high school years to work on a milk truck route, although I can't verify it. I do know for a fact that he had been injured while in the Army. I had heard my parents discuss the metal pin in his leg, and occasionally I have noticed his slight limp. But I believe the accident was the consequence of a convertible and an off-duty pass, not an enemy skirmish. I know he was stationed in Korea for a while. I know he enlisted in the Air Force after a few stints in the Army. He became a military career man.

Because Robert spent the better part of my childhood away from Michigan—in places like Korea, Germany, the Netherlands, Alaska, South Carolina—he has always impressed me as being more of an uncle than a brother—a munificent uncle to be sure, but an uncle nonetheless. A distant uncle. An uncle who, during a rare visit, would gift his nephews and nieces (my children) gargantuan bags of bulk candy—gummy sharks or licorice whips—for no reason other than he was able to. An uncle that would overdo Christmas by giving everyone frivolous electronic games and toys no thrift-minded parent ever would.

The kind of relative that, when we hear he has developed cancer, we find ourselves empty of the kinds of feelings we should be feeling because we haven't been as familial as we should have been. So we are struck suddenly with emptiness and guilt—emptiness for the opportunities for intimacy that we never sought out, and guilt for our waiting too long to seek them.

It occurred to me during the 1980s that everyone has a cancer story. Obits citing death from one form of cancer or another began to appear with regularity in local and regional newspapers, or, in the case of prominent citizens, on TV and radio newscasts; cancer among celebrities began to generate scores of biographies, even award-winning movies. Written tributes to cancer victims became so common that they evolved into a distinct literary genre.

Whole communities began gathering in 24-hour fund-raising events for cancer research and survivor tributes, and to give testimony to the sadness and overwhelming humanity we each must suffer in our dealing with an untimely death by cancer. Cancer was a topic at every meal with my in-laws; my father-in-law would lose his decades-long battle with oat cell cancer within months of my brother's diagnosis (—not a surprise, really, given my father-in-law's chain-smoking and alcoholism, lifelong habits he abjectly refused to abandon). In such a culture of cancer, my brother's diagnosis of inoperable brain cancer—at age fifty-one—was hardly new or unusual.

But he was my brother, and for that reason I felt . . . it is difficult now to say what I felt. I suppose I wanted to feel sad, to feel horrible about the loss I would suffer. The loss I was *expected* to feel—it occurs to me—by a culture that perpetuates industries of loss-acknowledgement: cancer research, treatment, support, and sympathy. While I knew very little about him, Robert was, after all, my brother, a blood relative.

A distant uncle.

I mean to write a tribute here, in the manner of, say, a eulogy or remembrance. But I do not have much to go on, my recollection of Robert so scattershot and second-hand that it may as well be composed by a ghostwriter. I hesitate to share the most personal and vivid memory I have as it is not one that would likely generate much sympathy, not even among cancer survivors. It would not put him in a good light—in contrast to what tributes are wont to do. Instead, to write about my eldest brother, I'd have to address America's hypocritical attitude toward social acceptance in the 1950s, especially as it relates to our country's fascination with cigarettes, and I'd have to mention Robert's mean approach to discipline.

Not only was smoking considerably more acceptable in the 1950s than in the 1980s or 1990s, it was also stylish and fashionable. My mother smoked L&Ms for years (despite her repeated claims—after quitting cold turkey upon her doctor's warning—that it wasn't *her* shown smoking in the family films of holiday celebrations). My father smoked cigars when he worked in the yard or was out fishing. (There were cigarette ashtrays on every coffee and end table in our Bloomfield Hills residence, but *cigars* were not allowed in the house.) During family get-togethers, which my parents often hosted (due to the available space—and the *lake*), the house would fog up with smoke and ashtrays would every so often need to be emptied. Our home movies show most of my aunts and uncles—and brother Robert—smoking. For impressionable children of the time, the fascination with putting burning objects in the mouth was inevitable.

Robert was babysitting the afternoon that my brothers and I decided to find out what the interest was all about. "Babysitting" meant that he pretty much left us alone, unless we got hurt or threatened each other with some weapon. He probably spent the time watching Soupy Sales on TV. "Finding out what all the interest was" meant that Kenny and Dick and I went out behind the garage to smoke. I was five or six; Kenny is just over a year younger than I am; my brother Dick is two years my senior, give or take.

We acquired the matches easily; all we had to do was move a magazine or two on the coffee table. But getting something to smoke was more difficult. We first tried long pieces of dried grass, pulled up from where the lawnmower didn't get close enough to the garage. We pretended we were Indians smoking the Peace Pipe. The grass tasted a lot like the burning barrel where Dad cremated paper plates and Dixie cups after a weekend gathering. We then tried rolling up pieces of newspaper, but they burned too hot and too fast. Finally, one of us snuck into the house and climbed on the kitchen counter to get in the cupboard over the refrigerator. Robert was probably alerted by a "Nothing!" answer to his question "What are you doing?" because we barely got the pack of cigarettes open when he came storming around the old dog pen at the back of the garage.

"So you want to taste cigarettes?" he said, and he grinned.

We knew immediately that we had sunk deep into trouble. But no one would have imagined at what cost.

My brother's punishment for our attempted smoking was to force-feed each one of us a cigarette—to make us eat it. I don't remember actually swallowing, but to this day whenever our road is freshly tarred or I happen to drive past coastal oil refineries, I am reminded of our punishment, and I can feel the acrid, leafy burning in my gums. I'm sure I was spitting out pieces of tobacco for weeks—brushing it out of my teeth for months. I also can remember being isolated in my bedroom all afternoon with the biggest stomach ache I've ever had. I don't recall eating dinner that night.

Except for a brief, ill-conceived attempt ten years later, when I sought to hang out with some older high school students that I thought were "cool," I have never tried smoking again. Even to this day, when I see someone with a wad of tobacco in his lip, I gag. I can't watch baseball very long for that reason. Cigarette smoke in restaurants turns my stomach (a culinary liability during the years we lived in Europe). When the Surgeon General confirmed that some forms of cancer could be attributed to smoking cigarettes, I wasn't surprised at the least. (What continues to baffle, however, is how many people choose to ignore the surmounting evidence . . . It's the same people, I believe, we're meant to empathize with during Relay 4 Life.)

My brother may be just another statistic. He took up smoking unfiltered Lucky Strikes or Camels in the Army (so he says, though he may well have been a smoker in high school, as early as the afternoon when he was babysitting). He smoked for more than thirty years. While I can give him some credit for my own aversion to smoking, for my relative health consciousness, I must also acknowledge that he himself chose to ignore the very lesson he meant to share. I've always suspected that at some time during his thirty years of smoking he developed cancer in his lungs, which then spread to his brain.

I'm not blaming cigarettes entirely. There have no doubt been a number of factors in my brother's hard life that may have contributed to his cancer—stress, an excessive fondness for Stroh's, poor nutrition, lack of exercise. Even his job with the military, which was secretive and may have involved long exposure to radio or "micro" waves, may have played a role. But at this point, the cause is irrelevant, the effect the same: my brother died much younger than he should have. And I can't enlist any more emotional response than what might be rendered by a medieval *danse macabre*: The most vivid memory I have of my brother involves *damnation* and *punishment*.

In the 1980s, each time my wife Debbie and I talked about having another child—of which there are now four, in the same gender order of my brother Robert's four (boy, girl, girl, boy)—my mother (who raised six kids) seized the occasion to remind us that *More is better.* "The older ones take care of the younger," she said.

Nothing could be truer—or more regretful.

AUG • 63

II.

No amount of intelligence prevents one from being stupid.

DIVING LESSONS: A MEMOIR

What I Remember Most

Five bodies crammed in a dull red '67 Volkswagen Beetle hurtling through the darkness of Grand Traverse County, Michigan. At least one of the bodies is wet from skinny dipping in Spider Lake (mine); others are dampened by late summer humidity and/or nervous sweat. Some of the skin in the car is more tacky than wet, chilled by shock, disappointment, anger, or the diuretic of too much alcohol. No one is speaking. The attempt to tune in WCCW on the AM radio with the broken knob has failed. But it's just as well. With the windows in the un-air-conditioned car rolled down, even rock & roll would be difficult to hear above the whine of tires, the whoosh of night washing around the sail-shaped window vents, the static of crickets and frogs.

I am driving, though it's not my car, and in spite of the general acknowledgment among the other passengers that I have just been injured. Maybe seriously. My forehead is bleeding; the left pocket of my short-sleeved madras shirt contains the fragments of more than one of my teeth—those that were not spewed into Spider Lake during the short, violent rant of curses that I'd performed. I am driving not only because I am now the most sober person in the car, but because I am the only one who can drive a stick.

We are headed to someone's aunt's house. Once there, I'll drink another Southern Comfort and Squirt while someone's aunt, a school nurse, will clean out the lake-bottom grit from the most obvious of my wounds—a one-inch scrape on my forehead, at the hairline—and where I'll assure everyone that I'm really all right, except for the cracked teeth. No big deal. At least one of the shattered incisors had been an oft-filled baby tooth anyway, as it was a genetic trait of my father's side of the family to not develop certain permanent teeth, among them incisors and the far back molars called "wisdom teeth."

Days later, I would question whether my lack of *wisdom* teeth had in fact precipitated that night's stupidity.

What I May or May Not Remember (The Next Morning)

Sobbing. For my stupidity. For my punishment. For my reckless, mistaken love. For my selfish and hurtful arrogance. For my drunkenness itself. For my uncertainty in 'forcing the overwhelming question.' ['Do I dare?' And, 'Do I dare?'].[1] For my [prescient] sober embarrassment. For my *parents*' embarrassment (—I, the "golden boy" of their six children, according to my sister Margaret). For the lessons I had taught but apparently not learned myself, even as I was just then embarking on what would become a teaching career. For my inability to impede the sobbing. For coveting the wife of my best friend. For my jealousy and anger. And—just possibly—for my pain, as the alcohol was wearing off.

But not, sad to say, for the awareness of my brush with death. That would come later.

What I Barely Remember

More than two hours in Dr. Shipley's dental chair as he extracted shards of teeth from my gums. Shipley's office was attached to his home on Peninsula Drive, a half mile or so from Traverse City Central High School, from which I had graduated five years before. (Someone's niece—at whose house I'd apparently spent the night—had driven me to Dr. Shipley's, once I got my sobbing under control.) While I had not visited the dental office with any regularity since going off to college, Dr. Shipley had been our family dentist for so long that he was willing to see me as an emergency case despite it being Labor Day Weekend. After excavating the ruins of a set of teeth he had spent years maintaining, Dr. Shipley filed down the rough spots on the teeth that still might be saved—temporarily, at least.

I would return in two weeks for him to begin reconstruction. (And continue appointments biweekly for the next few months, then once-a-month for well over a year.)

When the good dentist had finished fixing what he could, I was so groggy and numb that I was unable, without help, to lift my head from the dental chair. I assumed it was due to the immoderate amount of Novocain that had been necessary. But Dr. Shipley thought otherwise. He suggested that a trip to the ER at Munson Hospital was in order.

What May or May Not Be Some of the Facts
(That Were Clarified Much Later)

"Cervical spine (C-spine) injuries," reports Dr. Igor Boyarsky, in an online article on C2 Fractures, "are the most feared of all spinal injuries because of the potential for significant deleterious sequelae. Correlation is noted between the level of injury and morbidity/mortality (i.e., the higher the level of the C-spine injury, the higher the morbidity and mortality)."[2]

For many years after my skinny-dipping farce, in the rare, intimate moments that I overcame my humiliation and confessionally exposed my drunken folly, I claimed the break was at C2, for that's what I seemed to recall being told. Then, in my early sixties, when I underwent an MRI for symptoms that my physician thought may be related to past injuries, the nuclear med technician could see no evidence of damage at C2 but thought that C5 showed scarring. My request for records from Munson Medical Center in Traverse City, to verify the exact location of the fracture, proved fruitless. Because I had not been formally "admitted" to the hospital—the injury was treated in the emergency room and then I was referred to Dr. Clark, an orthopedic surgeon—no patient intake forms, no X-rays, had been retained. Instead, the only copies of records that were located by the staff at Munson Medical Center (and forwarded to me) documented the treatment of my multiple-fractured left shoulder, which had been the result of another impetuous, youthful stunt, for which I was hospitalized during the final three days of Advent in 1963 [and another story entirely].

Much of the current information about cervical fractures is now found at sports medicine websites, for the simple reason that such fractures are most often caused by a forceful impact, or traumatic blow to the head, and that "impact sports, or participating in sports that have a risk of falling or 'snapping' the neck (skiing, diving, football, cycling) are all linked to neck fractures."[3] Consequently, the C-spine industry has expanded exponentially over the past three decades as sports participation has burgeoned at every level (individual, community, school, professional, and semi-professional). The treatment for a broken neck, however, has not radically changed since 1973, and "depends upon which cervical vertebrae was damaged and the extent of the fracture. A minor (compression) fracture is often treated with a cervical collar or brace worn for six to eight weeks . . ."

I wore my brace for the better part of three months, almost to Thanksgiving. Still, the treatment suggests my broken neck was not too serious, more likely C5 than C2.

The Depth of Spider Lake at the Point of Impact

I would claim, in my occasional recounting of the incident, that the depth of the water I dove headfirst into was "six inches." Witnesses would argue eight or ten. No one ever suggested that it was deeper than a foot. I can recall wading back to shore after the accident—cursing and screaming, and fishing pieces of teeth from my mouth—with the surface of the water barely reaching my shins. Days later, physical evidence suggested that the water was shallow indeed. While most of the initial triage had been directed to my bleeding skull and mouth, I later discovered abrasions on my knees, shins, and the top of my feet as well.

When Asked Why

My roommate John, a biology major, would occasionally store his homework in the apartment fridge our senior year of college. Consisting of a cat carcass—or, at times, a dog shark—the relevant parts of a dissected and plastic-bagged body were labeled with small, crimped, color-coded slips scripted in difficult handwriting: lungs, kidneys, heart, muscles, arteries, nerves. Other than the six-packs of beer we would run "over the hill" to get for the weekend (Boyle County, Kentucky, being dry), John's cadavers were often our only cold storage.

What the separate parts were called was easy. Even I, an English major, outperformed the average score on the mock GRE's in biology (John and I exchanging our tests for the fun of it; he outscored me in literature). But ask how it all functioned together, and more often than not some visiting fraternal wit would retell the old joke about dismantling an engine to see how it worked and, after reassembling it, having parts left over that didn't seem to fit.

"What have we got to lose?" I would tease. "When you're done studying, let's put the cat back together, hit it with jumper cables, and return it to the alley, to live with the other strays."

I have provided a similar response—facetious and deceptive—whenever I'm asked why I dove into the shallows of Spider Lake in the first place. The fact is, I knew better. I had taught swimming for years by then—diving do's and don'ts—and had included on the written portion of the test I gave to my Junior Lifesaving class what I thought was an obvious question: "*True or False*: You should never dive into unfamiliar water."

But logical explanation, it seems (or even a philosophical explanation, for that matter), has yet to account for youthful abandonment—our risk-ripe adolescence stretching into our twenties like an elastic launcher of a balsa airplane. Especially in the America where I grew up—*Mid*western, *mid*dle class, *mid*-twentieth century—and where the prosperity of post-war economics, combined with parental leniency, tended to delay one's maturity. (Some called it *privilege*; others called it *spoiled*.)

"Boys will be boys," it's often said, assigning a gender-specific excuse to youthful transgressions. Others (my mother included) have been known to apply the seemingly forgivable catch-all of *boys will be bored*. Still others argue it may be genetic, a mutation of male DNA.

In other words, there may not be a single explanation.

One Explanation

I was not a typical high school student—if "typical" is defined by the teenage characters portrayed in popular novels, films, and locker room apocrypha of the 1960s—at least in terms of the consumption of alcohol. I did not break into my father's liquor cabinet and steal off with my buddies to some ramshackle fort to get stink-faced. Nor did I ply the "loosest," most well-hung girl of my 10th grade class with vodka filched from the bottle stored in the out-of-reach cupboard above the refrigerator—and then re-line with tap water, so no one would know—in order to impress her (i.e., cop a feel). Throughout high school, I felt a certain moral superiority to such immaturity. I did not need to drink to get a buzz on (I argued); my life already presented me with enough hormonal ups and downs that no other stimulants were necessary. In other words, I was pretty much a dweeb. Even throughout the better part of my college years I did not drink—let alone do other drugs, which were coming into popularity (and readily available) about that time.

As for other vices: I had "tried" cigarette smoking as a sophomore in high school, just as I had, about the same time, tried-out for the tennis team. In fact, it may have been the influence of other members of the tennis team that mitigated the smoking, as I was not any good at tennis and, by way of prior embarrassment and humiliation, not particularly fond of competitive sports in general (not to mention bending to the authority of peer pressure). I soon quit both. Tennis took practice, I discovered. And after an exceptionally vomitive poker party (involving cigars), and a certain incident with an orange-hot, free-ranging cigarette among the upholstery of a Ford Mustang traveling about eighty-miles-an-hour along M-22, I became prudish about smoking. Even (some might say) preachy. With minor exceptions, I became a goody-two-shoes to the extreme. Consequently, I couldn't imagine I'd be drinking alcohol until I was able to do so legally.

I started in Europe. I was twenty, a junior in college, and spent the winter term of 1971 in Paris, studying French language at the *Alliance Francaise* and, at the American Centre, studio art—sculpture, to be exact, working with a Romanian artist who had been a disciple of Brancusi. Paris being what it is, and artists (and students) what they are, and the cost of beer or wine more affordable than bottled water, and the "drinking age" in France somewhat amorphous—I began drinking alcohol in earnest.

Once back in the States—either in Michigan (my parents' residence) or in Kentucky (where I attended college)—I was close enough to the legal age (twenty-one in both states at the time) that I often wasn't ID-ed, not to mention that everyone I knew (my roommate John, in particular) was already old enough to buy. Consequently, my twenty-first birthday, in November of 1971, was anticlimatic—just another day of the week.

But then—and this is where I could easily place blame if I were inclined to—on New Year's Day of 1972, the legal drinking age nationwide was reduced to eighteen (in conjunction with the reduction of voting age). Suddenly, the world as I was beginning to know it—bars and parties and attention being paid—was rich with three-years' worth of (legally) inebriated women testing their sexual freedoms and maturity.

I suppose one could argue that my burgeoning and extravagant enthusiasm for alcohol at the time may in some ways have been a subconscious attempt to catch up on what I felt I had missed during the temperance of my high school years. Or maybe it was a sign of the liberating times—the political backwash of the Women's Lib, Civil Rights, Free Love, and Student Power movements of the late 1960s. Or perhaps it truly was genetic and I was just a late bloomer.

A Vague Memory That May or May Not Be Genetically Relative

My grandmother Urquhart's cottage was reputed to be one of the earliest summer residences on the south shore of Big Platte Lake in Benzie County, Michigan. The cottage was located on Bixler Road, adjacent to the Bixlers' own place. Mr. Bixler was a kind, friendly, unpretentious overseer of sorts, given to hailing summer mornings by the ringing of a farm bell at exactly 8 a.m. In addition to his cottage, and perhaps a few rentals along the shore, Mr. Bixler owned several acres of property on the non-lakefront side of the road, including a large field of randomly-spaced evergreen shrubs, which he took pains to keep mowed and trimmed, though the parcel seems to have served no other purpose than as a playground for vacationing children. The field was a perfect arena for hide-and-seek, our nightly entertainment during the weeks my cousins and I spent together at my grandmother's.

Lake access for the renters at Johnson's Resort bordered the other side of grandmother's cottage. The small cabins of the resort itself were across the road. In contrast to Mr. Bixler's benevolent amicability, Mr. Johnson was an ogre. More than once when we were playing baseball in the open lot adjacent to the cottage, old man Johnson would step out of the second floor balcony of his house and yell at us—"GET OUT OF THERE, YOU ROTTEN KIDS!"—which sent us scurrying through the cedars that defined the property line. (Only much later would I come to understand that Mr. Johnson's vehemence was nothing more than gimlet-enhanced teasing.)

After my father bought a cottage of our own on Platte Lake, a mere quarter mile away, I'd stay at my grandmother's only on occasion, as for sleepovers when Mr. Bixler's grandsons were visiting (Brad Bixler being the same age as my cousin Nancy and me). My grandmother, in fact, had begun to spend less time at the cottage, having gotten to the age (and health) where she seldom desired—or was able—to spent the entire summer "at the shore" nor had much interest in making the six-hour drive from Detroit by herself; as a result, my aunt Sue and uncle Nelson (Sue being my mother's younger sister) began spending more time there. A physical education/health teacher and textbook salesman (respectively), they had liberal summer vacation time. Uncle Nelson, in fact, had taken over the care and maintenance of the cottage and begun to enlarge it, as the two small bedrooms were insufficient space for three teenage daughters, let alone additional cousins. We began to call the cottage "Sue and Nels'."

My cousin Nancy, the youngest daughter, was my age, having been born just three weeks before me. As a result of our age and family proximity, Nancy and I spent pretty much every summer day together—swimming, boating, fishing, riding bikes, lounging on the dock, or, if the weather was rainy, playing board games, Chinese checkers, or cards. But after dark, after hide-and-seek, we'd generally find our way back to our separate cottages and our own beds. Except for the occasional sleepover.

It was during one of those rare cousinly sleepovers at grandmother's cottage that I was awakened in the middle of the night by the sounds of a struggle: grunting and moaning, shushing noises, cabinets bumping, screen doors clacking, curses. At first I'd wondered if the monster raccoon we'd seen rifling through the garbage cans the night before had somehow gotten into the kitchen and was frolicking among the leftover snacks and treats we adolescents had disorganized on the countertops. But when I stepped out of the storage-cum-sleeping room to investigate, I found my older cousins standing in the kitchen watching my drunken uncle trying to wrestle my drunken aunt into the house. There seemed to be an argument going on as to how it should be accomplished—one person applying more physical force than the other person thought necessary, and so resistant to the idea, etc.—though I'm not sure that either one of them even knew what the ultimate goal was. It was my first experience with "falling down" drunks. One of my older cousins entreated me—repeatedly—to go back to bed. "It's nothing to worry about," she said, in what I would later recall as a strangely unaffected voice. So I took her advice.

In the morning, nothing about the incident was mentioned.

What May or May Not Be the Taste I Remember

In the instance of driving one's head into the bottom of Spider Lake with such force that one's tongue is permanently "tattooed" and several of one's teeth are fractured like parish headstones subjected to a sledgehammer, the result is a blend of several distinct tastes: the chalky meat of an over-baked largemouth bass that was lured from beneath a swag of lily pads in a slow-moving muck-bottomed pond; the gritty marl that covers every fallen branch, clam shell, or stone in a river-fed lake, like those we'd collected as boys and scraped to reveal the iconography of fossil; the rust of iron, as from seldom-used cottage water pipes or long-exposed ship cables; unoiled oarlocks; the "rainbow, rainbow, rainbow"[4] of gasoline suspended in the unbailed water of an aluminum fishing boat . . .

What American Beer Tasted Like in 1956

My mother would have seen it as a familial or social responsibility, given our economic position; my father would have seen it as a marital consequence. As a result, in the late 1950s, my parents often hosted family or neighborhood parties at our rambling lakefront house on Middlebelt Road in Bloomfield Hills. Thanksgiving, Christmas, Fourth of July, Labor Day. A good number of these gatherings were recorded on sixteen millimeter film—my father had the latest equipment—and in many instances those films have come to serve in place of my memories of the seven years we lived there (from the time I was one until I was eight).

My parents were not drinkers, although they felt compelled by their position as upper middle class to socialize, and so my father often had a beer or two as host. He also would allow us kids a small sampling, in the bottom of a five-ounce Dixie Cup (which we would retrieve from the dispenser next to the bathroom sink). As Bloomfield Hills was a suburb of Detroit, he often drank Stroh's—"supporting local," as we now say. Stroh's had a taste like no other beer (the best-selling at that time being Schlitz, Blatz, or Pabst), though to be honest I wouldn't have been able to distinguish differences. To me, Stroh's had the color and carbonation of Vernor's Ginger Ale—another Detroit product—which I often (play-acting) claimed was beer. But there was an odd, uninhabited-room taste about it as well—not unlike my grandmother Urquhart's cottage—a musty, old newspaper taste, with a fragrance of insect casings and water from a neglected hand-pump. And then an aftertaste: the fishy porch screens of a morning on the lake after a rain.

We were living in that house on Pine Lake when my oldest brother Robert, immediately upon his graduation from Bloomfield Hills High School, enlisted in the Army. Given what I now know about my brother, it's likely that he had begun to drink beer while still in high school. And it's even more likely that it was Stroh's, the brand he was faithful to right up until his death from cancer in 1991, a few months shy of his fifty-second birthday.

What Comes to Mind Now

At the time I entered Centre College as a transfer student in 1969, the phys ed requirement consisted of two units, which could be selected from a variety of courses. I was able to satisfy one of those requirements by teaching a Junior Lifesaving course for the Boyle County American Red Cross, Centre's natatorium being the only indoor pool in the county at that time. It was a win-win situation, as I needed to teach at least one course a year in order to maintain my Water Safety Instructor (WSI) certification, and I had no intention of returning to another summer of life guarding and swimming instruction at Elmwood Township beach near Traverse City, which I had done the two summers prior. While I wasn't very keen on teaching in a *pool*—to someone who grew up on lakes, the deliberate and limited length and width of such a "body" of water was constrictive, less than invigorating, not to mention chemically hard on the eyes and hair—I nonetheless thought it would be an easy way to get phys ed credit without having to participate in any team or group sports (which, as a result of several painful high school shower room experiences, I had aversion to).

To satisfy the second requirement, I took a diving class. I was a passable platform diver, having begun as a fearless eight-year-old launching myself headfirst off the upper dock at Beulah Public Beach, and then honing my jackknives and swans from various freighter "pilings," both active and abandoned, that serve as reminders of the glory days of Great Lakes shipping. Much of my life-guarding job at Elmwood Township beach, in fact, consisted of deterring risk-takers from climbing up and diving off the pilings at the coal docks, which were adjacent to the public swimming area. They were dangerous: weathered telephone-pole-sized posts thrusting up from broken slabs of marine concrete and wound together with disintegrating, tetanus-rich iron cables. Yet no sooner was the beach closed for the day—or whenever "business was slow" (that is, when no one was looking)—we lifeguards were the ones out on the pilings, propelling ourselves toward who-knew-what.

Of springboards, I had very little experience. I could cannonball from the one-meter board with the best of them or, with any luck, draw the attention of bikini-clad onlookers with a vast array of "crazy" dives (developed in my youth by meeting any challenge set up by my brothers on those rare summer travels when the family stayed at a motel with a pool and diving board). But springing to do a backwards summersault caused me some trouble. And my first attempt at a forward flip off the one-meter board smacked a certain amount of confidence right out of me. As a result, the three-meter springboard was more than I wanted to handle. While eventually I was able to complete the minimal requirements for the course—I could do a passable backward pike, but my forward one-and-a-half was nothing to store on film—I decided to stick with solid surfaces. The edge of a pool, say, or a sturdy dock.

More than once during my time at the Boles Natatorium was I encouraged to join the Centre College swim team, and each time I refused (see "aversion to team sports," above). But I'd often thought that some of the encouragement to join the team stemmed from my notable execution of a racing dive, which was, as they say, *awesome.*

What Has Come to Mind Periodically
in the Intervening Years

Lines from Adrienne Rich's Poem "Diving into the Wreck":

The words are purposes.
The words are maps.
I came to see the damage that was done
and the treasures that prevail.[5]

The Moment I Wish I Could Have Captured and Retained

In the air after I'd left the dock but before I'd hit the water. At that moment, I was fearless; I considered myself in peak physical form—unencumbered by (possibly mischosen) fashion, confident (in my diving abilities), knowledgeable (that I would draw attention, make a "splash" [so to speak]), and, by all accounts, attractive to the person I wanted to impress (someone's niece). The future was spread out before me like a sixteenth century geographer's map of the world. I was single, educated [sic], had money in the bank (from a summer's occupation as a potato chip distributor), and had just finished my first week of teaching as a graduate assistant at Central Michigan University. I drove a sporty Plymouth Barracuda, had recently acquired a very cute puppy ("chick magnet"), and shared an apartment close to campus with a young man who was seldom home. Life, as they say, was good. In that air—the warm, moist, cricket and frog sung air in which I was suspended (however briefly)—I had no reason to think that it could get much better. The stars shone numerous and bright; the night was beautiful; I belonged to it.

Would that I could have stopped time then! If for no other reason than as a reminder of how indifferent and fragile our lives actually are.

What I Remember Saying Moments Before

"Is it deep enough to dive?"

"I don't think so," said a voice.

"Probably a couple feet, at most," said another voice.

"Not a good idea," said a third.

"Not even a racing dive?" I said.[6]

My Father in Abeyance

I have in front of me a two-and-a-half-inch-square black-and-white photo of my father diving off a raft in Platte Lake. The picture is dated August 1963, and my father is caught mid-dive, suspended, which is fairly remarkable given the technology of photography at the time. The photo was taken with a simple Cub Scout camera that had been given to me by my Aunt Mary—my father's only sister—the year before. What possessed me to take the snapshot is the fact that I had never seen my father swim until that day—let alone dive—and I was astonished by it.

Years later, when I discovered this photo in a box of childhood mementos I'd left in storage, I rediscovered my astonishment, so much so that I was moved to try and record it in a poem:

Wave-laced Platte Lake lacks color,
a steelhead gray in black-and-white,
while the bold horizon's forest of pine
and State Park campfire smoke closes

dark and unfocused on the hottest day
of August 1963. The day of my father's
last swim. What compelled him then
even now isn't clear—he refuses to say—

a man more known to love the faster waters
of a trout-packed stream. And how
I happened to have my Cub Scout Kodak handy
seems miraculous.

Perhaps he only thought to catch—
what I on the dock must have thought

as he splashed half-laughing up at me—
the trout-quick silver of a perfect moment.[7]

My father's splashing up at me was captured in another photo, which shows a playful smirk on his face—the closest thing to a smile he was ever willing to share.

In that respect, I am said to be like my father.

Platte and Spider Lakes Compared

The bottom of Big Platte Lake varies depending upon where along the shore you are. To the east, where the Platte River empties into the lake, the bottom is black-silty and bog-like, what I always think of as "brackish," though mostly for the sound of the word, as I am aware that the proper definition of *brackish* denotes "containing salt; briny" and there is nothing salty about Platte Lake. Instead, the bottom along the eastern shore, as I remember it, was mostly what we boys called "mucky": dark, fine, easily disturbed sediment, "teeming" (as they say) with aquatic life. The small bay where the river enters the lake was a prime location for bass, turtles, and frogs, what with the rich abundance of fallen cedar and pine trees in various stages of rot and molt (detritus of extensive logging), not to mention a Monet-envious engorgement of lily pads. Just east of the mouth, where the North Branch of the Platte River drains from Little Platte Lake (and slows to the point of being called "The Deadstream"—the local road named for it), the current was so reduced as to be easily maneuvered in a fourteen-foot rowboat with a ten-horse outboard. In the bay, the movement of water was negligible. If not for an occasional breeze, one could cast for bass among the lily pads there without need of an anchor.

Along the northwestern shore, where the river empties from Platte Lake and commences a jaunty, reckless journey to Lake Michigan, the water flows more rapidly, reducing the bottom to bright, gravelly, mostly golf- and baseball-sized stones, interspersed with an occasional cotter-pin-shearing rock. By the time the river reaches the big lake, it's mostly sand. More the fast, clear habitat of trout and smelt than that of bass or turtle, the river's relentless and heady escape from the deepest part of Big Platte Lake allows very little sediment.

The southern shore, where my father bought our cottage, was "rocky," though three sections of dock would generally get one out into what Mark A. Tonello calls "predominately sand, with large stretches of gravel shoals."[8] Our "beach" was more like gravel shoal: stones of various sizes, commingled with clams and clam shells, snails and snail shells, deadwood and reeds, and other forms of natural debris, generally of a uniform color (grayish/green—the term "uniform" being used ambiguously here), encrusted as it was with what seems to be properly called "marl."[9] As such, being of uncertain footing and slippery, and mined with penknife-sharp fragments of mollusks, the shallows were not swimmer-friendly (thus, the dock), though it was, for young boys, a veritable playground, rich with water life and other forms of entertainment. I would spend hours fooling around in the shallows, scooping up crayfish from their hiding places, netting minnows, antagonizing clams.

My brothers and I understood that there was to be ABSOLUTELY NO DIVING in the shallows nearest shore, even if our dock did not have the painted warning which some neighbors' docks did. If I had ever suggested doing something so crazy as diving into the shallows, my mother would have—in the words of another old joke—killed me.

In contrast, Spider Lake is best described as a spring-fed, clear-water, all-sports lake. Its name (I would guess) stems from the many thin "arms" or bays that tentacle from the main body, making the lake seem smaller than what it is. The popularity of Spider Lake, its densely situated, family-friendly resorts, have perpetuated a significant number of boating regulations (wake, noise, etc.), which have secured the lake's attraction. Many of the resort pictures at www.spiderlake.org indicate that much of the shore is mostly sand, with no more than small stones scattered about. Unlike the dangers of Platte Lake's gravelly shoal, the soft sandy bottom of Spider Lake would likely give a little when struck with a dumb object. Which probably saved my life.

The Element of Water and Its Role in the Narrative (Part I)

Suspended between manifestations of earth (rock, sand, silt, vegetation, flesh) and of air (cloud, sky, wave, snow, breath), infused with them, water is ambivalent, a suspension of contraries, of condensation and vaporization, of comings and goings, of life and death.

An Aphorism That May Have Been Inspired by the Spider Lake Incident

"Left to our own resources, we will waste them."

An Alternate Explanation: Signs (Early and Late)

I was born in November, a Scorpio. The eighth sign of the zodiac, Scorpio is governed by the planet Mars, though its principal star is Antares ("anti-Mars"). "Traditionally," writes Hans Biedermann, in *The Wordsworth Dictionary of Symbolism*, "Scorpio has been associated with male sexuality, destruction, the occult, the mystical, illumination—and, to offset the arachnid's venom ... healing and resurrection. In this way even a potentially dangerous sign is understood as ambivalent: a source of change, a symbol of the triumph of life over death."[10]

"The Element associated with Scorpio is Water," writes the author of the Scorpio page at *Astrology.com*. Yet, "As opposed to the 'roiling seas' seen in other Water Signs, a better motto for Scorpios would be 'still waters run deep.'"[11]

The Element of Water and Its Role in the Narrative (Part II)

> "In many myths of the creation of the world, water is the primordial fluid from which all life comes, but it is also the element in which creatures drown and matter dissolves. ... This elemental symbol is highly ambivalent, since it is associated both with life and fertility and with submersion and destruction."
>
> —Hans Biedermann, *The Wordsworth Dictionary of Symbolism* (trans. James Hulbert, 1992).

13 Ways of Looking at a Near Death Experience
That Does Not Result in Religious Conversion
(With Apologies to Wallace Stevens and God)[12]

1. "When I consider thy heavens, the work of thy fingers, the moon and the stars, which thou hast ordained; What is man that thou art mindful of him?"[13]

2. "The mind is its own place, and in it self / Can make a Heav'n of Hell, a Hell of Heav'n."[14]

3. "What is the good of your stars and trees, the sunrise and the wind, if they do not enter into our daily lives?"[15]

4. "O my God, what am I / That these late mouths should cry open / In a forest of frost, in a dawn of cornflowers."[16]

5. "As he rose and fell / He passed the stages of his age and youth / Entering the whirlpool."[17]

6. "'I have no desire to walk on water,' said Siddhartha."[18]

7. "If you choose to get yourself into trouble, you are smart enough to get yourself out."[19]

8. From "One Speaks of Penance":

> *—not a god's voice, though we'd have thought so*
> *at first—but a voice of all*
>
> *we did when we shouldn't have, and all we knew,*
> *and, in that knowledge, all we expect to be told again,*
> *desperate to hear what we've already heard,*
> *to hear a voice from somewhere*[20]

9. "[T]he blank, unholy surprise of it."[21]

10. What is a lesson, if not a threat to what we believe?

11. "Karma," says Jane.

12. No amount of intelligence prevents one from being stupid.

13. Only eternity endures.

Abeyance, Ambivalence, Ambiguity: The Question of Word Choice in the Narrative, and, by Consequence, a Defense of Connotation in Memoir

In drafting the section of this essay that describes the moment I wish I could "capture and retain," I originally used the word *abeyance*, which, according to my somewhat dated *American Heritage Dictionary* (1969), is defined as "the condition of being temporarily set aside; suspension." Yet the semicolon in that definition implies an equality between those two meanings that, to me, doesn't exactly jibe, since "suspension," as I understand it, has a certain intensity, an immediacy, that I would not reckon with something "set aside" (in the sense of abandoning or neglecting). The definition itself then is somewhat inexact and, as such, is connotatively more along the lines of what I meant when I used the term *abeyance* as the title of a series of short poems that I had written between the years 2000 and 2006, or thereabouts.[22] Each poem in the series is exactly 140 syllables and linked one to another through thematic and formal conventions, though line and stanza lengths vary; each poem attempts to capture a sonnet-like moment of "suspension," the apex (so to speak) of one juggler's ball: the moment between tossing and catching, between beginning and ending, between attraction and rejection. A pause at a moment in which pause is impossible (i.e., after my feet lifted from the dock and before my head plowed into the lake bottom).

And yet, as I think about it, that particular moment is not so much the apex of a juggler's ball, really, as it is the arc itself, the line connecting one point to another, a line that was in my case imperceptively arced, as my dive was meant to be shallow, like a racing dive, almost skipping into the water.

"It was a good dive," said Dr. Clark, the orthopedic surgeon who read my neck X-rays. "Straight on. A slightly different angle and you'd have been dead."

The capture of such a moment, then, is less *abeyant* than it is *ambivalent*, the term Hulbert uses in his translation of Biedermann's discussion of water as a symbol (earlier); *ambivalence* is defined as "the existence of mutually conflicting feelings or thoughts, such as love and hate *together* [my italics] about some person, object, or idea,"[23] a term (appropriately enough) coined by Freud.

The element of water is *ambivalent* then, both life-giving and life-taking; the astrological sign of Scorpio is *ambivalent*, in its tendency toward destruction and resurrection; the coexistence of damnation and salvation in Christian theology is *ambivalent*; in psychology, the ego and the id are *ambivalent*. Good *and* evil. Real *and* Ideal. Then *and* now. Birth *and* death. Brilliant *and* dumb.

Fiction *and* Non-.

Life is itself a suspension of opposites, or contraries, leaving us with a variety of meanings, of explanations, of causes *and* effects, in constant flux; *ambivalent*, and consequently, by the nature of language, *ambiguous*.

Two Views of Covetousness Introduced and Compared (as a Mitigating Factor in Cause/Effect Analysis)

If one believes that my injury was the result of the life I was living at the time—a warning, if you will—then one must take into consideration which sinful behavior(s) may have brought me to the attention of a punishing God.

The first that comes to mind is lust, though *lust* itself is a connotatively ambiguous word, engendering, to me, a certain amount of physical evil, along the lines of Lotharios and date rapists. Even considering the implication of *lust* in the "goat-footed balloon man" of E.E. Cummings' poem "Chansons Innocents: I,"[24] which suspends the reader in the ambiguous lechery of a "mud-luscious" encounter (i.e., the urgings of fertility and promise in the more innocent reading of the poem; the danger for Betty and Isabel in the more suggestive), I would dismiss *lust* as a possible antecedent to my misfortune. My sin was less of the flesh than of the mind.

At the same time, I will confess more than a few instances of *covetousness* in my youth and young adulthood—not so much of material possessions (*covetous* and *avarice* used interchangeably in some discussions of the Cardinal Sins)—but of girls (later, wives) who "belonged" to some of my friends, acquaintances, or colleagues. [The term of possession is not mine; the era of which I speak was 1970s Feminist.] In my case, I tended to covet relationships I could not have; I was attracted to girls/women who were not available. Moreover, I may have been attracted to them *because* they were unavailable. And while such a concept may be deemed sinful in the context of Christian morality, the practice itself has become one of the primary themes of American literature and culture (as exemplified, over and over, by writers like F. Scott Fitzgerald, by Hollywood film productions, and by a myriad of twenty-first-century television dramas). In those few instances where the individuals I coveted eventually came within reach, became "available," so to speak, I found myself backing away; I was no longer interested.

Covetousness, then, may be a sin of perpetual realignment in the free market world of consumerism, the way that disappointment is an unyielding consequence of desire. It's in our Capitalistic nature to *want* (more, newer, better), and yet our *having* is often less than satisfying. The thrill is in the challenge, not the victory. Accomplishing our goals, achieving our dreams, acquiring property—leaves us purposeless. Without purpose, we have no life.[25]

The dragon of covetousness, however, has a legendary second head that engenders many noble features. What comes to one's literary mind is "courtly love" as it is manifest and defended through much of English literature since the twelfth century (and later adapted, popularized, and promoted in American culture as *romance*). Courtly love is described as "true" love, in that it often transcends the (legal or religious) formality of marriage; despite its "adulterous" implications, writes Peter G. Beidler in *Backgrounds to Chaucer*, true love "can endow a man with nobility of character," causing even a selfish person "to perform many graceful services" in honor of his beloved.[26] To a modern reader, stories that exemplify courtly love include Sir Gawain and the Green Knight, Tristan and Iseult, and the Arthurian legends (especially involving Merlin, Lancelot, and Guinevere—or at least Disney-fied versions of them), among others.

Andreas Capellanus is acknowledged as establishing the "rules" for courtly love in his medieval Latin text *De Amore* (*The Art of Courtly Love*),[27] despite the fact that his "rules" are more the observation of principles than they are guidelines or recommendations. Covetousness is knightly, we're told, and thus it is not too much of a stretch of the imagination to see my youthful, fumbled moments of showing-off as acts of courage and bravery, done to ennoble myself to (or to honor the whim of) some "beloved." After all, "Marriage should not be a deterrent to love," writes Capellanus, and "Good character is the one real requirement for worthiness of love."[28]

This ambivalence of covetousness has unfortunately perpetuated its association with other sins, which, in certain circumstances, may be indistinguishable. We may covet another person's wife for our own *lust*ful pleasure, or we may covet her as a way to displace our *envy* (of the person whose wife she is). Which may also cause *anger*:

"Why that jerk?!" Or violate our manly *pride* and as a result provoke more damning actions, like vengeance, murder, torture . . . well, you get the idea.

As for me, there was seldom anger involved. I did not place blame elsewhere. My covetousness was selfishly romantic.[29] It was more about overcoming what I socially and competitively saw as injustice or unfairness ["Why *not* me?"], and which I now believe is just foolish egoism: quirky, evolutionary humanness. As we develop within the species, different situations provoke different emotional responses, some of which favor certain individuals expressly (for one reason or another). We are moved to act, or react, almost as if for the action itself—as if the self is spurred at the sudden thought of selfhood, or the soul at its awareness of soulness. And while we would like to believe we have a certain control over some of those situations, most of them are unaccountably random, the result of—what?—shifts in atmospheric pressure? Artificial stimulants? Natural selectivity? Predestination? Social media?

Who knows. Surely some of my readers—those who believe in the deliberate administration of an all-powerful overseer—will argue that my near miss of death (of an untimely final dowsing) would suggest that I was spared—or saved—for some *purpose*, and that, if so, then God is benevolent and merciful, not punishing.

While I personally—to this day—cannot find such beliefs existentially viable, at the same time I do not dismiss the viability of such a possibility for others.

Narrative as Resurrection (And/Or Redemption)

In discussing the authenticity of Jesus's words and stories as they are recorded in the New Testament, biblical scholars

G. Earnest Wright and Reginald H. Fuller summarize: "Behind the words . . . and the memories about him—even behind those words and memories whose authenticity is doubtful—there shines forth a self-authenticating portrait of a real person in all his human uniqueness, an impression which is accessible alike to the layman and to the expert, to believer and non-believer."[30]

I have used ellipsis in this quote to indicate my redaction of the prepositional phrase "of Jesus," as the comment could just as easily be made about *anyone* whose existence is substantiated through fiction, memoir, or oral tradition. Narrative is self-actualizing. And yet, as it often involves rewording or refashioning one's "past," we are also transcended from it, albeit imperfectly.

Memoir is, at best, more *portraiture* than history.

The Element of Water and Its Role in the Narrative (Part III)

Those readers who know my theological eccentricities (practicing Presbyterianism, say, without professing it) may be wanting to dismiss the biblical discussion above as disingenuous; they will moan and boo audibly in the essay's arena. Those who know my poetry, on the other hand (and my fondness for ambiguity and metaphor), will take up their paper megaphones and chant: *BAP-tism, BAP-tism, BAP-tism.*

A Brief Early Attempt at Rendering the Incident into a Prose Poem (With the Working Title of "Skinny-dipping")

"This story then," said the girl, "about breaking your neck so many years ago, diving into a shallow lake at night when you were drunk—six inches of water!—despite the fact you knew better, having taught water safety for years—this is not a story you now think is funny?"

"No," he said, with barely a smile.

Notes

[1] T.S. Eliot, "The Love Song of J. Alfred Prufrock," in *Selected Poems* (NY: Harbrace, 1936): 12.

[2] http://emedicine.medscape.com/article/1267150-overview (accessed 21 January 2013).

[3] http://sportsmedicine.about.com/cs/neck/a/neck5.htm

[4] Elizabeth Bishop, "The Fish," in *The Complete Poems* (NY: Farrar, Straus and Giroux, 1969): 50.

[5] Adrienne Rich, "Diving into the Wreck," in *Poems: Selected and New, 1950-1974* (NY: Norton, 1975): 197.

[6] In retrospect, my inexact presence of mind would render the question moot.

[7] Titled "Evaluating a Photograph," it was first published in *Lucky Star* (1.4: 1983). The issue in my possession indicates that Lucky Star was a production of Erie Street Press out of Oak Park, IL. The editor claims a 'one-man' operation but does not give his name.

[8] "Status of the Fishery Resource: Platte Lake" (Department of Natural Resources, July 2010); www.michigan.gov/document/dnr.

[9] According to Britannica.com, "marl" is an "old term used to refer to an earthy mixture of fine-grained minerals. The term was applied to a great variety of sediments and rocks with a considerable range of composition." As a boy, I didn't know what to call that yucky stuff

that collected on everything along shore; all I knew is that it was pasty and khaki-colored and would get under our fingernails as we unsettled rocks looking for crayfish. Tonello himself uses the term marl to describe "the remaining deep water areas" of Platte Lake, citing as his source H. L. Seites' "Inland Lake Survey: Platte Lake 2009."

[10] Hans Biedermann, *The Wordsworth Dictionary of Symbolism*, translated by James Hulbert (Ware, England: Wordsworth Reference, 1992).

[11] http://www.astrology.com/scorpio-sun-sign-zodiac-signs/2-d-d-66949

[12] I use the term "God" in the broadest, most metaphorical sense yet encourage the reader to interpret the reference in the way that is most comfortable to him/her.

[13] Psalms 8:3-4. In *The Holy Bible: Containing the Old and New Testaments; Translated Out of the Original Tongues and With the Former Translations Diligently Compared & Revised; Set forth in 1611 And Commonly Known as the King James Version.* (This particular edition was presented to me at the Kirk in the Hills Presbyterian Church [Bloomfield Hills, Michigan] in November 1959.)

[14] So speaketh Satan in *Paradise Lost* by John Milton (http://www.gutenberg.org/ebooks/20).

[15] Margaret Schlegel, in *Howards End*, by E.M. Forster (1910).

[16] Sylvia Plath, "Poppies in October." The poem is dated October 1962, the month Plath separated from Ted Hughes. 1962 was also the year of her son's birth (in January), of a contract for the publication (in England)

of *The Bell Jar*, and of the composition of many of her most anthologized poems, including "The Bee Meeting," "Lady Lazarus," "Daddy," and "Nick and the Candlestick," among others. Plath committed suicide in February 1963.

[17] T.S. Eliot, "The Waste Land" (lines 316-318 [Section IV, "Death by Water"]).

[18] Hermann Hesse, *Siddhartha* (New Directions, 1951).

[19] An aphoristic paraphrase of the brief advice given to me by my father in the spring of 1967, upon my return from the Jackson (MI) police station, where Mike and I had been detained for loitering and vagrancy. We'd hitchhiked from Traverse City to see a girl I had met at the State Park the summer before; we'd hitchhiked partly as an adventure and partly because my driver's license, which I'd possessed for barely six months, had been suspended as a result of an extraordinary speeding ticket. Framing this advice in an aphorism seems appropriate here, as it mimics the wisdom one finds in the Biblical proverbs, which are themselves based on ancient forms, according to Wright and Fuller in *The Book of the Acts of God*: "Both Egyptian and Israelite wisdom sayings are in the form of a large variety of short, epigrammatic, poetic lines that are sharp, to the point, and easily memorized. Furthermore, the form in which they are given is the speech of an old man to a young man, the former sharing his wisdom with the latter" (Anchor Books, 1960; p. 192).

[20] First published in *The Dickinson Review* 11 (1997), under the title "Penance, and the Nature of Ventriloquism," I probably composed the poem about 1990, though the earliest record I can locate is dated 9/2/1991, under the

title "The Voice Discovers Penance," as part of a series I was working on at the time (*The Discoveries of the Voice*). The complete poem can be found in *Local Congregation: Poems Uncollected 1985-2015* (Main Street Rag Publishing, 2023).

[21] Spoken by Macaulay Connor in *The Philadelphia Story* (1940). Connor (played by James Stewart) has seen the "magnificence" beneath the hard, "goddess" exterior of Tracy Lord—her "flesh and blood," her "hearth fires and holocausts." The ambiguity of the lines suggest that social flaws (superiority, privilege) are, at base, human flaws, and therefore not surprising at all.

[22] Winner of the Frank Cat Chapbook Award in 2007, and first printed in a limited edition of one hundred copies, *Abeyance* appears as Section II in *Local Congregation* (Main Street Rag 2023).

[23] *The American Heritage Dictionary of the English Language* (1970).

[24] http://www.poets.org/viewmedia.php/prmMID/15398

[25] "Life is indeed dangerous," writes E.M. Forster in *Howards End*, "but not in the way morality would have us believe. It is indeed unmanageable, but the essence of it is not a battle. It is unmanageable because it is a romance, and its essence is romantic beauty."

[26] Peter G. Beidler, *Backgrounds to Chaucer* (especially "Chapter Ten": www.the-orb.net/textbooks/anthology/beidler/courtly.html.)

[27] "Rules of Courtly Love," at http://web.cn.edu/kwheeler/rules_of_love.html.

[28] "Rules of Courtly Love," cited earlier.

[29] And if I distilled anger in someone whose girlfriend I might have "stolen" (temporarily)—should you be reading this—I'm sorry. It was, as they say, nothing personal.

[30] *The Book of the Acts of God* (Anchor Books, 1960): 265.

0 9338

III.

Eventually the rain stopped, and though it was still quite cold, we spent an enjoyable afternoon roaming the marketplace and bolstering our Christmas spirit. We bought Santa hats.

STÖLLEN

Flour

Four hours after its predicted arrival, the storm settles in. As usual, my mother takes to baking. And I help, if for no other reason than first dibs on a lickable beater. I crack eggs, or sift the Gold Medal through her antique sifter, triggering with double grip the handle that spins thin blades across screen. *Sift. Sift. Sift.* It is the sound my black boots make, much later, when I march through certain textures of snow.

Eggs

Biology was required my sophomore year in college. Labs consisted of cell classification, reproductive anomalies, ova. In no time yolks began to glaze over, stare mindlessly toward the ceiling . . . [And who would have guessed then that years later I'd paint a room the color of yolk?—Only to repaint it when I found the tint too much like the wallpaper in Gilman's story, which I'd also read in my sophomore year.] We opened shells at various stages, examined them, scoped the spermy embryo, the small soft bones that Vietnamese (we were told) fried and ate as a delicacy. To this day, I can barely do much more with eggs than use them for baking.

Butter

The buffet at Crystal Mountain Resort was enchanting after a long day on the slopes. All-you-can-eat. Thick soups, salad bar, pasta—a complete and separate table laid out with large servings of cakes, pies, ice cream sundaes. Rachel, in particular, having followed-the-leader with Kids Club instructors down the Bowl a dozen times, anticipated the dessert choices. Yet no sooner did she return to family seating with an exquisite tiramisu than our waitress intercepted it: "Display only." It was one-of-a-kind, sculpted out of animal fat, gelatin, and food coloring. A horrible embarrassment for a girl known as "exceptionally bright," it was also a defining moment for her. She would study to become an artist, then a pastry chef. Now she bakes organic bread, the kind that tastes better without anything on it.

Milk

In the U.S. Department of Agriculture *Farmers' Bulletins, Nos. 301-325*, published in 1908, F.O. Foster, an instructor in dairying at the Michigan Agricultural College, confirms that the method for developing cultures of bacteria as described in "Practical Use of Starters in Ripening Cream" has three advantages:

The starter can be kept for a much longer period, thus saving one-half or more of the cost of pure cultures.

The milk is always ready for inoculation and the mother starter can be transferred each day when in the best condition and kept vigorous.

In case a starter is not needed every day, the mother starter can be carried along conveniently without the trouble of storing milk.

In 1910, F[loyd] O. Foster married Maud Sterling. In 1914, the couple gave birth to a son, James, who would later become my father. In 1918, after Maud was killed by a freakish automobile accident, James and his baby sister Mary were taken in by Maud's brother, Clarence, and his wife Margaret and raised as their own. A few years later, my father, James Foster Sterling, had his names changed legally, inverting the middle and the last. I never met Floyd Foster. But late in the 1960s I learned that the person I called Grandfather Sterling, whose middle name I share, was, in point of fact, my great-uncle.

Sugar

In the early 1960s, my family lived year-round in a small "winterized" cottage on Platte Lake. My parents indulged me during those years, in part due to the remoteness and relative isolation of that dwelling. One Spring, my mother said that if I collected enough sap, she could make maple syrup. I hung coffee cans on two of the maples in our yard and then tapped as many trees as I could (undetected) on the private, seasonal properties up and down Carter Road, with framing nails bent to direct the drip. In a week, I had a couple gallons, maybe. My mother boiled the sap all day on the stove, reducing it to one serving for pancakes and a leftover teaspoon of what she called *candy*.

That was the same year I spent days writing my first "novel," a sappy story about a solitary child who asked for nothing more than a sibling for Christmas (and who was—surprisingly, magically—gifted with an adopted brother). My father typed it for me: two pages, single spaced. In point of fact, I was fifth of six children and had to share a tiny cottage bedroom with two annoying brothers.

Yeast

According to joyofbaking.com, the word "yeast" comes from the Sanskrit 'yas' meaning "to seethe or boil." It is a living organism, a single-celled fungus belonging to the *Saccharomyces cerevisiae* species. In order to grow, yeast must have three things: moisture, food, and warmth. For that reason, it generally prefers women to men.

Salt

In the pleasures of childhood before memory, or rather in the pleasures *beyond* my father's 16mm home movies, which have come to form the basis of my earliest memories, my mother piloted a group of Cub Scouts through a tour of a salt company somewhere in Michigan. I can recall the coastal, salt-fogged air of an enclosed warehouse, the size of which I'd never seen before, and a mound of rock salt rising like a dingy ski slope all the way to the ceiling. Was it the Detroit International Salt Mine, a primary supplier at the time? It must have been around 1958, the year that the Morton Company produced a short promotional film, *White Wonder*, which claimed that there are 14,000 uses for salt. (Now available on the Internet, the video, one reviewer notes, is "a marvelous stroll through all sorts of 1950s culture.") But I can't be sure. There is no photographic evidence of my visit.

Water

In Poland, most schools—and many businesses—are closed on Easter Monday, or *Smingus Dyngus*, a day when men and boys are traditionally encouraged to douse females with water, using whatever is available: cups or pitchers, buckets, squirt guns, even garden hoses. While predominantly aimed at girls of child-bearing age, there are no statutes of limitation on the soaking. Some believe the tradition to be of pagan origin, as water has been considered for centuries a purifying source; others trace the practice back to Prince Mieszko the First who is purported to have had his entire court baptized on Easter Monday in 966 A.D. In 1998, when we lived in Lublin, my fifteen-year-old daughter Sarah thought the holiday was "stupid" and "unfair" (even "sexist") and so, in an act of what may be considered true "cultural exchange," she launched water balloons from our balcony onto the unsuspecting boys roaming *Park Akademicki*. Retaliatory assaults escalated into a full-fledged, block-long, international water fight—curses echoing in several languages—an experience Sarah now recalls as "cleansing."

Cardamom

"A stimulant and carminative, cardamom is not used in Western medicine for it own properties," says *The Epicentre: Encyclopedia of Spices*, "but forms a flavouring and basis for medicinal preparations for indigestion and flatulence using other substances, entering into a synergetic relationship with them. The Arabs attributed aphrodisiac qualities to it (it features regularly in the Arabian Nights) and the ancient Indians regarded it as a cure for obesity." In baking, cardamom is best known for its use in Dutch "windmill"-style cookies and certain recipes for hot cross buns, both of which bring to my mind the season of Spring. My mother baked hot cross buns every Easter, though I was well into adolescence before I made any connection between her method of frosting and the

Presbyterian symbol for a Risen Christ. (And well before I recognized the funny irony of serving lamb for Easter dinner.) Windmill cookies remind me of the Netherlands, which we visited periodically in 1993, especially the Keukenhuf gardens, as lush and brilliant an account of resurrection as is earthly possible.

Cinnamon

The older I get the more I become like my mother, which is unusual only to the extent that I'm a male progeny, not a daughter. (That I'm *not* her daughter, in fact, may well be the reason why I'm willing to admit I'm becoming *like* her . . . something my sisters would not likely do.) If domesticity is genetic, my predilections might be more readily traced through my mother's family, the Urquhart clan [its castle on the rocks of Loch Ness, near Drumnadrochit] than through the Fosters or Sterlings. I prefer the kitchen to the garage and would rather bake peanut butter cookies than go fishing. I add cinnamon to my French toast because my mother made it that way. Much of what I learned about baking (or sewing, or childcare) I learned from my mother. In contrast, my father, whose Scots ancestors likely skirmished with Urquharts on more than one occasion, never slathered his French toast with syrup, as we kids did. Instead, he seasoned it with salt and pepper. "It's just eggs," he said. "You don't put syrup on eggs."

Note: My well-worn copy of *Betty Crocker's Cookbook* (revised edition) makes no mention of cinnamon in the recipe for French toast (p. 30)—nor vanilla, for that matter, which I also use when making French toast, the way my mother did.

Vanilla

I've never been convinced that "Imitation is the sincerest form of flattery." To me, such an idea speaks more of plagiarism than profundity, and I seldom hear the saying repeated without a hint of sarcasm. [Consider, for example, the tonal modalities of synonyms for *imitate*, as defined in *The American Heritage Dictionary of the English Language* (1969): *mimic, ape, parody, simulate* . . .] The exception is vanilla flavoring, which, in imitation form, has all the qualities of *real* vanilla at, as they say, "a fraction of the price."[1]

Orange Zest

The outermost parts of lemon or orange rinds contain oils that are intense with flavor and are therefore occasionally used in recipes to add "zest," as in piquancy. Other definitions of *zest* include "spirited enjoyment; wholehearted interest; gusto." In consequence, one could readily use the term to describe the Mardi Gras *cortège* in Binche, Belgium—which dates back to 1549 [some say]. Different groups of "Gilles," dressed in matching jester-like outfits (replete with bells), march in their wooden shoes up the main street and through the town square, their slow progress marked by a dirge-like beat of drums and by a barrage of blood oranges flung into the crowd, as well as against storefronts and houses. (Upper windows are often covered

[1] Quotation marks are the definitive punctuation, when it comes to sincerity. Using them, I acknowledge that the phrase is borrowed, and that I am intentionally imitating advertising copy for effect. Had I left the phrase unquoted, the reader, in recognizing its cliché-like familiarity, may have inferred a joke, a sophomoric irony, and, consequently, dismissed the whole paragraph as insincere. On the contrary, not only do I buy imitation vanilla but choose generic or store-brand labels whenever possible.

with fencing or shutters, to prevent breakage.) If one is attentive and lucky—as my children Andrew, Sarah, and Matthew were when we visited in February 1993—he or she can acquire dozens of perfectly ripe and tasty fruit in the process. But as with many *carnivale* celebrations, the Binche *cortège* involves much drunkenness and firecrackers and Silly String and aerosol cans of foam and retaliation and carelessness among the less than attentive crowd, which more often causes damage and injury, not to mention a great many oranges smacked against one's head or crushed against one's body and/or underfoot. At the end, Binche is a sticky scene of blood orange carnage and rind litter—though overwhelmingly aromatic. *Zesty.*

Candied Orange

In the summer of 1993, after my year's teaching at the University of Liège (Belgium), we decided to take advantage of "already being" in Europe by renting a car and spending a month or so touring. The "car" turned out to be a white, nine-passenger Ford minibus (diesel), the smallest vehicle available that could legally transport a family of six. Our first stop was Bork Havn, Denmark, where I'd reserved a rental cottage for a week. But it was not the beachside summer holiday we'd imagined. The only day we were not buffeted by brutal winds off the North Sea (not so good for sunbathing or biking, though great for windsurfing on Ringkoning Fjord) was the day we spent inland, at Legoland. It was that same evening, upon our arrival back in Bork Havn, when we stopped at the Sail Inn restaurant to see if they accepted credit cards, when a gust of wind ripped the driver's door of the minibus from my grip and slammed it into the car I'd parked beside, smashing the mirror and denting the side panel. I was in the process of leaving a note of explanation when the driver approached. I pointed out the damage. Clearly he was disturbed (it was his father's new car), though he eventually came to understand that it was merely an accident and that insurance would take care of it. There was not even a scratch on the minibus.

I was reminded of this incident last week, when—despite my extraordinary caution ever since—the door of my twelve-year-old red Ford F-150 blew open in the Walmart parking lot and left a prominent paint transfer on the polished passenger side of a silver Cadillac. This time, I acted as if nothing happened and drove off without leaving a note.

Choose the appropriate conclusion:

1) Dear Cadillac owner: I'm sorry. I'm a different person than I was in 1993, when it was my nature to model proper behavior for my children. (They've turned out fine.) These days I'm reeling from years of an all-consuming custody/parenting battle from a brief second marriage (and lengthy divorce) which has me at odds with the world. It has nothing to do with you.

2) I'm sorry, but these things happen all the time. (See above.) Try a good rubbing compound. You shouldn't have parked so close.

3) The color and shape of the mark on the Cadillac looks kind of tasty, don't you think? Somewhat like candied orange peel.

Currants

Not those of the species *Ribes* (family: *Saxifagaceae*), related to the gooseberry, which are, according to www.wisegeek.com, "thornless upright shrubs which yield glossy red or black berries." While the berries of that species are edible and occasionally used in cooking (or jam), commercial cultivation of red and black currants was banned in the U.S. until 2003, due to concerns that "they could harbor disease which had the potential to devastate American timber stocks." Instead, think Zante currants, cultivated for centuries in the Mediterranean, which are actually a small, seedless variety of grape (*Vitis vinifera*).

Cherries

I got my first real job at fourteen: picking cherries for a friend of my mother's, who had an orchard off Silver Lake Road, on the hill above where the new Traverse City Junior High would eventually be built. My mother drove me over in the morning and picked me up at night. We were paid daily, in cash, and while I thought that was pretty cool at the time, I realized later it was merely a way to avoid dealing with work permits and taxes.

Black sweet cherries ripened first, and at first we ate nearly as many as we picked, climbing the pointed ladders into the branches or, in my case, up the trunk and out the limbs, more than a few of which broke off in my attempt to get to the highest. With the exception of a few migrant families, the picking was mostly done by kids my age. (It was years before the popularity of dwarf cultivars; mechanical harvesters were a recent development and expensive, used only for sour varieties, which ripened later.) For weeks my hands were stained the color of the ink holders some of the desks at the old junior high still had.

I was diligent at first, tireless. But when I began to notice how the girls from St. Francis High School would laugh as they worked in adjacent trees—how different they seemed out of their pleated-skirt uniforms, how personable, how their shorts and bare legs became smudged with tree bark, how their hair curled in the gray humidity or fixed suggestively to their sweaty foreheads and cheeks—I began to dawdle and goof around. I joined in the windfall fights. And yet, when two or three of the girls would sneak off to the pine lot, taunting and giggling, and two or three of the older boys would follow, I stayed behind, returned to picking, wishing it were me. (Oh, how I wished it were me!)

Golden Raisins

Six years after our parents died, my sister Margaret included with her Christmas card four of the recipes most commonly associated with our holiday gatherings: Mother's Cherry Squares, Aunt Sue's Green Salad, Grandmother Sterling's Raisin Custard Pie, and Grandmother Urquhart's Crumb Pie. Margaret had typed and formatted (centered) the recipes with her word processing program and then printed them in red-plum-colored ink on sheets of festive stationery (in the background: a New England village covered in snow, replete with a white steepled church; in the foreground: a horse-drawn sleigh).

The third recipe from the top looks something like this:

Grandmother Sterling's Raisin Custard Pie (my favorite)

8 inch baked pie shell (for 9 or 10 inch use 1 1/2 recipe)
1 cup seedless raisins (golden are nice)

1 cup milk
2 egg yolks (save whites for meringue)
3/4 cups sugar & 2 tablespoons flour mixed
nutmeg
Combine milk egg yolks, raisins gradually add sugar until it dissolves, cook over medium heat, stirring constantly until thick, cool pour into pie shell sprinkle with nutmeg.
Meringue: beat egg whites to foaming, add 1/4 teaspoon cream of tartar. Continue beating adding tablespoons of sugar gradually until peaks form. Bake at 350 degrees for 20 minutes until lightly brown

I recently found a copy of this document in the back of my cookbook. Of the four recipes, this one alone has penciled-in marginalia around it, all-caps, in a script I don't recognize: Above "(my favorite)" are the words "ABOUT 40 MIN PREP"; to the right, beside an arrow that underlines the parenthetical in the second line, the text reads:

DOUBLE THE RECIPE
BUT NOT THE SUGAR
OR RAISINS

And in the left margin:

ADD:
1 TSP VANILLA
PLUMP RAISINS
OVERNIGHT
IN SPICED
RUM

Cranberries

A. Because we always celebrated Thanksgiving at home as a family, I assumed throughout my childhood that side dishes like green bean casserole or relishes like homemade cranberry sauce (crunchy and seedy), which we only saw at holidays, were unique to my heritage, a tradition handed down from generation to generation. Not until I went away to college—so far away that my mother wrote on my early November birthday card "DON'T COME HOME FOR THANKSGIVING" and a boy in my dorm took pity on me and invited me to spend Thanksgiving Break with his family—did I realize that such specialties came in cans, with the recipe on the label (i.e., part of my "college" education).

Nevertheless, freshly made cranberry sauce was still a treat, though my non-partisan mother would insist that, for true democratization, we also have available the jellied form, which I would get the honor of preparing by opening both ends of a can, sliding the dark red tube of sauce into a blue antique relish dish, and slicing it into thick moons. Often the jellied cranberries would be left untouched until after seconds, just before pie, when my mother would rescue the deep brown hot-n-serve rolls she'd forgotten in the oven and I would use the cranberry sauce as jelly, helping to make palatable the overcooked rolls, one or two of which I'd consume, if for no other reason than to acknowledge my mother's good intentions. Overcooked rolls, served at dessert time, eventually became a holiday tradition.

B. Every morning my father would have a cup of instant coffee with his breakfast. Since my mother was not a coffee drinker, it made no sense to perk a pot of coffee just for him. She'd opt for tea—but only if the occasion called for something sociable and warm, something for which to pull out the china cups and saucers (like hosting Women's Circle from the church). Milk was the liquid of choice during meals (though it had to be in a pitcher; we could not put the bottle itself on the table), with the exception of breakfast, for which one of us would have to mix up some orange juice from frozen concentrate; otherwise, my mother drank water. Beyond meals, the primary drink—or addiction—was Pepsi. My parents' house was never without Pepsi. Pepsi was at the top of the grocery list every week; there were always empty Pepsi bottles in the entry, awaiting the next trip to the store. Pepsi was so much our primary recourse to thirst that its taste became redundant, even for my mother, who would occasionally be caught adding to her glass a shot of maraschino cherry juice or a squirt of Hershey's syrup.

It should not be too surprising, then, for me to acknowledge that on those rare occasions when my mother would splurge and buy some exotic foodstuff like Ocean Spray Cranberry Juice (this was years before designer juices became the fashion) I would mix myself a Pepsi and cranberry juice cocktail. Something I have a special affinity for to this day.

Almonds

There are few references to almonds in the Bible, in spite of the tree's Mediterranean nativity. Most notably is Genesis 43:11: "And their father Israel said unto them, If *it must be* so now, do this; take of the best fruits in the land in your vessels, and carry down the man a present, a little balm, and a little honey, spices and myrrh, nuts and almonds."[2]

---

[2] I quote from my King James Version, which, according to the inscription, I received from Kirk in the Hills Presbyterian Church on November 1, 1959. My name is embossed in gold-leaf on the cover. Its use here seems appropriate, as not only does the verse reference the gifting of almonds, but the story informs and furthers the history of Jacob's family (begun in Genesis 37). In a similar way, this particular bible informs and furthers my Scots ancestry: its progenitor, King James I of England, having ascended to that role from his former, as King James IV of Scotland.

The verse is primary to the story of Joseph—he of the dream interpretation [the seminal psychologist]—whose brothers, jealous of their father's partiality toward him, dispatch him to Egypt ("sell him" claim some versions), where he eventually finds favor with the Pharaoh. During the time of great famine in Canaan, the brothers are sent to Egypt to buy corn, where they encounter Joseph, though don't recognize him, and so he's able to engineer (through intimidation, hostage-taking, and threats) some convoluted "testing" of his brothers' filial devotion (and guilt).

In his *Illustrated Bible Dictionary* of 1897, Matthew George Easton clarifies that the almond tree's Hebrew name, *shaked*, signifies "wakeful, hastening," and was likely "given to it on account of its putting forth its blossoms so early . . ." As to Genesis 43:11, Easton conjectures that "[Israel] desired his sons to take with them into Egypt of the best fruits of the land, almonds, etc., as a present to Joseph, probably because this tree was not native of Egypt."

Whether the Biblical meaning accounted for my mother including almonds among the "special" mixed nuts she set out in wooden bowls for guests at Christmas time (along with the heirloom silver nutcracker and matching nut picks), I can't be sure. What I do remember is how, by Epiphany, only almonds and Brazil nuts would be left in the bottom of the bowls: Brazil nuts for their hard shell and bitter meat; almonds for their pocked ugliness.

Rum

My father seldom drank anything stronger than beer. And then only on occasion. My mother might have a "cocktail" during the holidays, but more so as a gesture of being the good host than because she had a taste for it. On those rare occasions, her preference was the daiquiri. Thus, the only hard liquor I ever recall finding in my parents' house was Bacardi rum, secluded behind the good china in the back of the sideboard. Or stored in the cupboard above the refrigerator, with other things that were seldom used, like the Universal Food Chopper No. 2 (an antique meat grinder), which mounted on the side of the counter or kitchen table and which my mother cranked by hand to make deviled ham.

Kirschwasser

The Christmas market in Aachen is typical of Germany: the main square and surrounding streets are filled with small temporary booths selling holiday craft items, gifts, and seasonal food—in gifts, everything from hand-tied lace, hand-blown ornaments, and delicately carved and painted wooden crèche figures, to plastic harnesses of sleigh bells and cheap felt Santa hats imported from some country where there is no snow; in edibles, everything from paper-cones of French fries (*frites*), or white sausages thrusting from wads of bread, to hot cider and wine. The day we visited—December 22, 1992—was cold and rainy, and we'd gotten there so early (to avoid the crowds) the only booths that were opened sold food. So we bought pastry for breakfast and hot wine to stave off the chill (even for the kids). When Andrew's lips began to turn blue, we sought refuge in a McDonald's, where we bought coffee and hot chocolate to sip while his shoes and socks were drying on the register. Eventually the rain stopped, and though it was still quite cold, we spent an enjoyable afternoon roaming the marketplace and bolstering our Christmas spirit. We bought Santa hats.

My journal from that day notes: "Bought a coffee cake/fruit cake like bread called stollen . . ." And that the exchange rate was "$60 = 90.90 DM." It also notes that I was enthralled by the cathedral, which was "near a toy store," especially when I learned it was at one time Charlemagne's palace church.

We'd tasted a variety of hot wines during the day—trying to stay warm—not to mention a number of other kinds of spirits. Whether any was the cherry brandy called *kirshwasser* (German for "cherry water"), I don't recall. There is no mention of that in my journal. But whenever I hear German spoken, or see a word like *kirshwasser*, I think of our visit to Aachen and the Christmas market.

Orange Liqueur

My "liquor cabinet" consists of a single shelf above the cereal shelf which is itself above the pantry where the spices are kept. Residing in the back of that upper shelf, behind the more cosmopolitan booze, is an odd assortment of liquors that have been left behind, often by members of my extended family, who most likely purchased the stuff during one holiday visit or another (unable, for one reason or another, to transport it home). A few have been in the back of the cupboard for quite some time, partly because I don't know what they might be used for (and so do not want to discard something that may eventually be needed) and partly because I like the exotic names: Blue Curacao, Crème de Cacao, Chambord, Schnapps. And their fancy bottles. One small squat bottle even wears a hand-knit stocking cap. The bottles lend a certain class to my cereal cupboard, which otherwise speaks simply of Kix or shredded wheat or Froot Loops.

Somewhere among those bottles is Triple Sec, which I know is orange flavored. I also know the label claims it is "the Brand Bartenders Trust" and lists the recipe for mixing a perfect Cosmopolitan at home.

Almond Paste

During the year I taught American Literature and Culture as a Fulbright Scholar at the University of Liège, our family lived in the Francophone region of Belgium. Thus, to foster "cultural exchange," as the Fulbright Program promoted, we enrolled our four children in a traditional and typical "public" school, the Catholic-sponsored St. Marie, where the language of instruction was French. We encouraged the kids' participation in all things *Belgique*. It was difficult, at first. But by December, they were fairly assimilated. With help of the other children on Rue Garde Dieu, they had written and posted letters to St. Nicholas, and so on December 6 we woke to find small boxes of candy and simple toys on our stoop (as did every child that provided the local mailman with an address, since "St. Nicholas" was a good will gesture of the postal service). Among the sweets was our introduction to marzipan, and the custom of shaping almond paste into traditional or decorative figures, including the Walloon folk hero Tchantchès, who is described in the catalog of the *Musée de la Vie Wallonne*, as "*petit homme aux traits rudes*." Tchantchès is a hard-drinking, carousing prankster, known for his (sometimes vulgar) out-spokenness and defense of individualism. Often dressed in the clothes of a common coal miner, he represents to many *Liègeois* the regional history of independence and self-reliance. His wife, herself both long-suffering and somewhat shrewish, is named *Nanèsse*.

"Liège is a symbol of rebellion against rule and regimentation," alliterates the 1992 Fodor's *Guidebook to Belgium and Luxembourg*. Yet the window display of a small patisserie near the Walloon Museum (which houses the Tchantchès marionette theater), offers marzipan in the shapes of Elmer Fudd and Spongebob.

THE PERFECT TREE

As a child, I believed in Santa Claus long after my more skeptical friends could prove that their fathers had amassed huge stockpiles of toys and gifts in the attic above the garage a few weeks before Christmas. And I believed in red-suited generosity and white-bearded kindness long after I discovered that my mother had the proper sales slips to exchange gifts that Santa had supposedly left in the wake of his whirlwind philanthropy. I continued to believe in Santa Claus even many years after the certain knowledge that my father himself played one of the starring roles in the December drama.

Santa Claus had a familiarity about him that convinced me he was real. I could never accept the fact that he was a stranger. He knew me too well for me to believe that he was one of the department store imposters who asked, routinely, "Have you been a good boy this year?" Their artifice was obvious—elastic and cotton beards, pillowed laps, *ho-ho-ho*'s that no imbecile would repeat as often. Those blatantly commercial Santas were just doing their jobs. The one photograph I still have of my brothers and me with Santa at Hudson's in Detroit shows his expression to be more of a forced grimace than a jolly smile.

Nor did the chorus line tap-dancing Santas on *The Dinah Shore Show* convince me that they were what they appeared to be. Female Santas in black leotards insulted my small intelligence. I knew that Santa, the *real* Santa Claus, like the Kris Kringle I'd seen in the movie *Miracle on 34th Street*, would not be so self-promotional, so egocentric, that he'd resort to performing little ditties on national TV. Those Santas were nobodies to me, and I couldn't believe that a distant and superficial nobody could make me feel so warm and mystified, so *Christmasy*. All along, I was convinced it was an inside job.

What kept me believing all those years—years that we lived in houses without chimneys—was the correlation in my mind of Santa Claus and fathers. While other children lost faith in their chubby hero when they discovered dear old dad munching on the bell-shaped cookies they had left for jolly old St. Nick, I believed more strongly. It was clear to me that the qualities Santa seemed to personify at Christmastide—patience, kindness, politeness, generosity—were the qualities of the best fathers all year long. And I took my own father as an example. Nothing that Santa did or could do was beyond my own father's capabilities, not even a little seasonal magic.

It was always after supper in mid-December, a week or two before Christmas Day, after we had been bathed and clothed in our matching Lone Ranger flannel pajamas, when my father would bundle his three youngest boys in winter coats and scarves, pile us with blankets into the backseat of his Mercury, and head down Woodward Avenue in search of what my mother called "the perfect tree." Those nights were always starless, as far as we could tell, lit up mostly by the streetlamps and the strings of white bulbs—brighter than any stars—that fenced in the used car lots where the trees were sold. The air was always dry and cold, blustery, and what meager drifts of snow may have accumulated were curled up like abandoned animals sleeping against the curbs.

The street would be busy, noisy, crowded, exciting. We'd drive past lot after lot jammed with trees—forests of Scotch pines and Douglas firs, blue and green spruces, red and white pines, and other evergreens that somehow seemed sadly misplaced in the grayness of the city. Car horns caroled out tunes if we slowed too quickly; at every lot PA speakers blared out scratchy renditions of "White Christmas" or "Jingle Bell Rock." When we'd finally locate the "right" lot—sponsored by my eldest brother's Boy Scout troop—the smells were smells of pine all right, but I could also detect grease and gasoline, exhaust, tar-paper, breath-mint (near the scoutmaster), cigar smoke, and chocolate.

By that time, my father himself would be filled with the spirit of Christmas. Normally a quiet and shy man in public, he'd suddenly be talkative and friendly, tell a joke or two (we could assume by the laughter), even laugh. Then he'd choose a tree carefully, eye it up and down, stand it on the sidewalk near the car for our inspection and approval, shake it and tap it to assure that all the branches opened fully, turn it, set it aside, and repeat the performance with another tree. From the car, where we had retreated to keep warm, my brothers and I would watch his tree-dance and nod enthusiastically at every choice. We'd yell "Yeah! Yeah! That one!" without really knowing what we were looking for. All we knew for sure was the pure, cold, tingling excitement of something very special about to happen.

After he decided, he'd pay more than what the tree was priced at, and then generously tip the scouts that tied it as best they could to the roof and trunk of the car. All the way home, he'd whistle the last carol he'd heard on the PA.

We'd go straight to bed, it being well past our bedtimes. Somehow our excitement was always tempered enough by sheer exhaustion that we would fall easily to sleep.

In the morning, the tree would be in the corner—in the space I now realize he must have had in mind all along—and it would indeed be *perfect*. It would reach almost to the ceiling, with only room to spare for an angel, and there wouldn't be a branch out of place, none too long or too short. It would seem as though the house had been designed for the tree; it was an excellent fit. Each year my mother would agree that it was the "most perfect" tree we'd ever had, and each year I was astonished at the small miracle of its perfection—the first magic of the Christmas season. Each year I was more convinced that my father, able to work such wonders, was Santa Claus.

Accepting this, I accepted my friends' silly skepticisms with smug complacency. Nothing else that happened during the holidays ever really surprised me, though it was still exciting to witness the magic *he* created—to marvel at how my father pulled it off, how he knew that I wanted a BB gun even though I never told anyone but Santa, how he was able to keep hidden from a boy's comprehensive house-search a four-feet-tall stuffed animal (a white monkey I'd call Flip), how he made it snow on Christmas Eve. By accepting belief in Santa Claus, I opened myself to all the magic and excitement of the season, and I was seldom disappointed.

My belief in a father/Santa figure lasted well into my high school years. In fact, as the years progressed, my convictions seemed to solidify and strengthen, to make perfect sense. What child does not wish to have Santa Claus as a father? He is generous to a fault, kind, understanding, gentle, and patient—he works magic. He is everything a child gets when that child's father plays Santa Claus during the Christmas season. Caught up in his role-playing, the holiday father spends time with his child, laughs more easily, gives (and gives in) more consciously, and spreads love and good will contagiously. Suddenly, the world is filled with Christmas. It made logical, practical, believable sense to me.

It was only after I married and moved away—and no longer made the journey "home" for the holidays—that my belief began to waver. My wife's Santa was a sad replacement; she worried about money and sizes and needs. Our inexpensive tree was a misshapen dwarf, a freak. It looked out of place anywhere. There was no magic. I began to fear that Christmas was only for children and that it would never quite be the same.

But I was wrong.

It was mid-December, a week or two before the first Christmas that our oldest child, Matthew, would remember, when I took him and set out with the sled to find what my wife Debbie called "the perfect tree." We went up to a friend's pine woodlot on a ridge overlooking a small lake in upstate New York, where we lived at the time. I had a corner of the living room in mind, and the air was primed for magic.

No sooner had we arrived on the bluff than it began to snow those slow, lazy flakes that seem to put everything in a different dimension, as though in liquid under glass. And as we watched the low clouds scuttle the distant hills, and as we listened to the quietude of our slight breaths, the snow filled our tracks, as well as those we had seen of deer, rabbit, and mice. Everything smelled like pine, sumac, wet sawdust, and candy.

Matthew was exceptionally jolly as I pulled him among the trees, eyeing certain ones carefully, merry-go-rounding others. It was not his first snow—he was just over a year old—but for some reason that afternoon I sensed that the snow made him especially tingly and excited. He tried to catch some flakes on his tongue, yet he seemed unconcerned whether he succeeded or not. When I tried, they were light and tasteless. But the looks on his face—the quick, bright smiles—made me laugh. Rosy-cheeked and cherry-nosed, well-padded in his snowsuit, hat, mittens, and boots, he looked himself like a small Santa. *Miniature sleigh and eight tiny reindeer*, I thought. Or, in our case, one huge man-deer.

We looked and looked. I shook the snow off some trees, walked around them, checked for short branches on others. When we found what I thought was the best of the crop—Matthew pointing: "Whadat!"—I cut it close to the ground with the bow saw, tied it to the back of the sled, and, with Matthew on my shoulders, we started for home.

Suddenly, two deer broke from the tree line within twenty yards of us. One quite smaller than the other, they appeared to be a doe and her yearling. They stopped, briefly, then two white tails waved good-bye. I could hear Matthew's quick-sucked breath, and I could almost feel his thrill.

That night, Debbie agreed that it was a perfect tree. There had been a couple short branches, but I put them against the wall, and, with a little pruning, there was room enough at the top for our angel. At least it was near enough to perfect so that Matthew wouldn't notice. And as I held him and looked at the lights reflected in his eyes—eyes seemingly the size of some of our ornaments—I could feel his whole body electric with pleasure and wonder, though I knew he wasn't sure why. He looked at me, to the tree, and back to me; he seemed to make a connection. Belief had been planted like a tiny pine cone deep in his small understanding. And *I* was Santa Claus.

FIELD CARE OF GAME

"A good knife and plastic bags are must items."
—Firearm Safety Handbook

The knife was new—a paper-sharp Camillus folding model with a three-inch blade. It had been given to me on my birthday just weeks before. And although my four children's names were scribbled on the card that came with it, I was fairly certain the gift was my wife's doing when I'd finally unworked the multiple layers of cellophane tape and year-old Christmas paper and found the thing. The kids had merely wrapped it and "signed" the card. I knew that none of them were at the age where they could afford such a lavish and lethal gift, let alone be legally able to barter their dimes and quarters at Al's Hardware and Sporting Goods in Canandaigua, where the knife was purchased, according to the address rubber-stamped in purple on the otherwise plain white box. Besides, I trusted that they knew better—even as infants—than to endorse recklessness on my part, given my history of miscarved Christmas roasts and Thanksgiving turkeys. Surely *they*'d be smarter than to supply me with such a dangerous implement, especially if they'd had any notion of what I was preparing to do with it.

Not that the gift wasn't attractive. Nestled in an orangish leather sheath, its rugged flap secured by a formidable brass snap, the knife not only possessed a uniform and manifest utility but also implied a kind of gendered artfulness; it was meant to hang with a certain manly confidence from my belt. Indeed, just moments before, I had unsnapped and unholstered the knife from its sheath, cupped it gingerly in my cotton-gloved right hand and with my ungloved left thumb jacked open the blade until it locked with a satisfying *click*. (I had also been careful, as my Boy Scout training reminded me, to keep the blade pointed outward and down as I did so.) Now, standing in the diminishing light of an unseasonably warm autumn day, I was able at last to admire more closely my heretofore unused gift.

The knife handle measured three-quarters of an inch at the front—the end from which the blade pivoted forward—and then widened lengthward with a slightly serpentine edge (for a more confident grip, I'd come to learn), all the way to the surprising crescent of its user-friendly butt end. It was aesthetically smart, a cherry-colored wooden grip riveted between handle ends burnished in nickel and bronze, the whole works finely-wrought and polished to a sheen. The blade, when opened, was engraved as *Sword Brand "Hand Made" steel*, and it narrowed from the handle to the tip with wicked precision, ending in a point that had been machine-honed to a sharpness capable of piercing the thickest deer hide.

Or so I hoped. For I was at that very moment standing above the awkward rumpled heap of a doe that in a few days hence—if the knife and I performed skillfully enough—would assume the unbodily form of forty-six packages of freezer-wrapped meat: a dozen chops from the sirloin (four per wrapper), several selections of broad flank steaks, and several dozen two-pound bundles of ground venison, each white, waxy-papered package distinguishable from its generic counterpart by the contents clearly labeled in black permanent marker.

But it was not a skill I had any practice in. I was placing a good deal of faith in the knife.

"I can do this," I said aloud, my voice tempered less by confidence than by strain. For the better part of fifteen minutes, I had been calling for Tom, my hunting partner, who shared the "group" doe permit with me and who had actual possession of the yellow adhesive tag we would have to attach to the hock of the deer's hind leg. No one had answered; no one was within earshot. Or else I was deliberately being ignored. Which, it occurred to me, was just as likely, especially given that what had begun as simple *halloo*s had fractured into a kind of hideous, wildly incomprehensible screaming at the loudest decibels my lungs could manage, which were considerable, to be sure, as they were driven by the flush adrenaline and crackly synapses of my first bagging of prey (albeit a doe)—what is otherwise known among the locals of Yates County, New York, as "kill thrill." I was fairly certain that in the process of my panicked yelling, I would have angered anyone attempting to stalk bucks within a two-mile radius, so much so that they wouldn't have responded even if they'd heard my pathetic pleas.

I'd concluded by then that Tom was likely positioned on the other side of the bluff from where I was standing, across Skyline Road, maybe down below my neighbor Burt's six-acre vineyard of Concords. Deer were known to be drawn there by either the loopy, tongue-memory of pilfered sweetness just before harvest or by the heavy-sugared ice-wine grapes that now dangled from the leaf-thinned vines like edible Christmas ornaments.

Either way, no answer meant that I was alone, as alone as a person could possibly be—a person, that is, who had just fired two slugs of a twenty-gauge shotgun into the neck of a formerly gracile creature, what my youngest daughter referred to generically as "Bambis." Never having shot anything dead before, I had fully expected, when the momentous time came, to have reveled in my success with a compatriot—slapped each other's backs heartily, repeatedly *Damn*-ed self-congratulations, and then saluted hunter kinship with a so-called field dressing—"saluted," that is, by essentially having someone else proceed in the postmortem dismantling of the thing, someone who had expertise in the matter. But since no one had answered my initial calls (not to mention my subsequent rants and curses), I was pretty much left to my own resources—*profoundly* alone—but for the ghost of an animal I had stolen life from half an hour before.

"I can do this," I repeated.

After all, hadn't I passed with some distinction the Firearms Safety Class that was required by New York State of all first-time hunters, no matter if they were thirteen years old or, as I was, thirty-one? Hadn't I tested perfectly on my knowledge of gun toting, fence crossing, unsafetying and firing? Hadn't I done respectably on the shooting range, blowing the hearts out of seven of the ten paper plates we'd (in simulation) hunted? Hadn't I taken proper notes when Bob ("Shorty") Johnson, our instructor, described the steps for field dressing, or "gutting," particularly heeding his warnings about violating the meat with intestinal bacteria? And hadn't I read and re-read the "Field Care of Game" chapter of my *Firearm Safety Handbook*, in the unlikely event that I would ever find myself in these very circumstances?

Besides, didn't a Ph.D. in American Literature suggest an above-average ability in comprehension and retention? Surely, people dumber than I was gutted deer every day. In theory, I understood what needed to be done, and I possessed what I needed to do it. In practice, I carried all the necessary equipment—a sharp knife, a plastic bag, a piece of string, a rope. Clearly, I was prepared.

But my tightened grip on the knife handle suggested otherwise. My hand had become unnaturally warm and sweaty, even numb.

Relax, I told myself. *You can do this.*

I opened my cotton-gloved fingers and looked again at my birthday gift; the unblemished blade spoke sharply, confidently: *You can do this*, it seemed to say. I grasped the doe's right hind leg with my left hand and jerked the carcass around in an attempt to reposition it from its haphazard heap, to spread open the legs and expose the soft white, light-haired underbelly, which suddenly reminded me of my dog, a mostly black terrier-spaniel mix, who would at times become matted between her legs and would violently resist lying still for me when I would use salon-styling scissors to remove the clumps and free her movement. I balked at the thought.

"I can do this," I said aloud.

"The animal's head should be pointed uphill," the *Handbook* had advised, ". . . so the entrails can be rolled out easily." Around me, the ground was mostly flat. Ever the good student, I yanked and dragged the deer by its foot until the body seemed to be at a slight incline. Then I released the leg. To my surprise, no sooner did I let go than the appendage folded back upon its counterpart, as if even in death modesty must prevail. I repositioned the head on its meager rise and yanked the legs open again—and again the hind quarters sprang shut. And a third time. Finally, I abandoned all hope of *properly* positioning the dead weight and simply jerked the bitch around until the legs splayed open.

"I *can* do this," I said emphatically. And crouched down by the doe's lovely tail, knife in hand.

WHILE ONE COULD ARGUE that I'd spent years preparing for this moment, one could counter-argue that any pause on my part was simply unreadiness. Throughout childhood and well into adulthood, I had been opposed to hunting as a sport. Granted, it was an opposition of sketchy rationale, founded more on a lack of exposure to hunting than on any substantive ethical principle, but I'd also come to consider myself by nature the kind of individual who would more likely open the window screen and shoo out the wasp than vacuum it to certain death with the Hoover. For one thing, there was no display of enthusiasm for hunting on the part of my early male role models, like my once upwardly mobile, suburban father. The only "game" he'd ever brought home to snippety Bloomfield Hills—according to family legend—was a pheasant that had run into the path of his pale green Hudson. My father had pulled to the shoulder of Middlebelt Road and retrieved the fresh kill. At home, he'd plucked its bright feathers and "processed" it, according to my mother, "just like a fresh turkey from the A & P." But apparently the fowl tasted wilder than what he or my mother had expected; the experience was mostly a disappointment.

Whether or not that single event in my family lore had anything to do with my father's subsequent disinterest in hunting, or whether he was simply more easily satisfied with fishing, a sport he was ardent about, I'll never know. His lack of interest in big game not only seemed to fuel my own disinterest but would eventually become the ethical basis for my anti-hunting stance. Or my ignorance. Except for BB guns at Boy Scout camp, the only shooting I'd been exposed to in my youth was that of my next older brother, Richard, who had at different times during the years we lived Up North taken his .22 into the woods and brought home squirrel pelts, which he'd stretched out on small homemade frames to cure (or dry) and then arranged on the floor of the bedroom, as one would a lion or bear skin. Pathetic little faux-trophies. For years, the image of those squirrel rugs on the floor beside my brother's bed represented to me all the silliness of tracking down and shooting game animals—large or small.

Even after my father fled suburban Detroit and relocated us to rural Northwestern Lower Michigan, where two-thirds of the students in the school I attended were absent on November 15 (Opening Day of firearm season), and the only topic of conversation around Thanksgiving was how many points a particular buck's antlers counted, I argued that such "sport" was fundamentally unsporting, given that it was hardly fair—a "hunter" with a high-powered rifle and scope pitted against a defenseless animal, who would, in fact, be lured within range of a deer blind by a pile of sugar beets.

I was nearly thirty when my opinion changed. At that time, in spite of my full time employment as an assistant professor of English at a small college in Upstate New

York, I had begun to find it difficult to clothe and feed our children, who seemed to be multiplying with some degree of regularity. The firstborn alone had placed my "family" on the eligibility list for some government subsidies, like fuel oil waivers and the WIC Program, which supplied "at-risk" women, infants, and children with vouchers for milk, cereal, cheese, and so forth. (Apparently, the average salary of a beginning English professor at a small private college automatically put his dependents in danger of nutritional deficiencies.) When our second child arrived sixteen months after the first, most meats, beef in particular—in the form of P&C's cellophane-wrapped packages of hormone-fed steer flesh—became an extravagance.

Fortunately, the word of my inability to provide adequately for my family spread among my rural neighbors, and we became the regular recipients of surplus venison. My neighbors routinely harvested more deer than they could ever consume themselves, and they encouraged me to take up hunting as well, which, for a meager fee (they argued), would not only supply the protein needs of my ravenous children, but would at the same time help my neighbors eradicate the ruminant pests from their vineyards, pumpkin patches, and buckwheat fields. Consequently, I felt determined to overcome any ethical opposition I had toward hunting and to take up the activity not so much for sport as for its practical benefits.

That's when I'd signed up for the hunting course. One neighbor loaned me a gun. Another gave me pointers on stalking versus standing; another, on patience and persistence; still another, on camouflage, Carhartts, and fox urine. Many of my neighbors not only gave me permission to hunt on their private lands but encouraged me to do so. Tom—whom I'd met when our wives found themselves concurrently pregnant and under the care of the same OB (and who therefore carpooled to Dr. Steadman's office in Geneva, twenty miles away)—applied for a group doe permit, listing me as his "group." Since females of the whitetail species were more plentiful and less wary, a permit that allowed one to shoot a doe pretty much guaranteed meat on the table. When deer season came in November, I was ready.

But not really, I think now. That first year I'd had several opportunities, took several shots, and quite possibly could have wounded a deer once, as evidenced by what appeared to be blood drops in the snow. But I'd not "bagged" anything. The only venison we put in our chili that winter was from the doe Tom shot (and shared), and what the neighbors gave us, either out of sympathy for my incompetence as a hunter or from a lack of room in their freezers.

In retrospect, I've often wondered if perhaps that first year I'd not been as ready to take an animal's life as I had thought. Sure I'd taken the course. Sure I knew what to do. But the fact that my shots *above* the back of a six-point buck, from a distance that, with my proven skill on the firing range, should have resulted in a winter's supply of venison sausage, suggested that perhaps my ethical sensibility unsighted my aim. While surely things were becoming more fiscally difficult for us at the time of my first hunting season, we had yet to see the birth of our third child, due the following January, and so hunting that first year was still more sport than necessity, more desire than need.

The next year was entirely different, however. I'd felt no compulsion at all firing a slug into the lower neck of a solitary doe, especially as it was getting late on opening day, the light coming low from the hazy west. My view from the toppled maple trunk where I'd stood, ten feet or so above the oak-leafed and fern-strewn ground, was diminishing, limiting my shot to twenty yards at best—still a safe distance for the small gauge Winchester I crooked in my arm. I'd had no moral twinge when I'd pumped another shell into the chamber and fired a second time. And I was elated—not disturbed—by the brief crackle and snap of underbrush, followed by the thud of a hundred and forty pounds of muscle and bone and blood dropping into the scrub brush this side of the marsh. I felt a certain pride in my role as provider, in the manifestation of my fatherhood and manliness. My strength and power. I'd felt pretty damn good.

But I was not prepared for the smell. I don't mean the initial smell of blood and feces, the whiff of deer beans that spilled from the anus when I finally thrust the tip of my knife blade into the short bright hairs of the butt, and then sawed around the sphincter, which I had intended to loosen from the muscle with my scalpel-sharp birthday gift in order to tie off the colon, so that, when I slit the sternum, I would be able to remove the intestines and entrails without fouling any meat. I had no intention of reducing the amount of chili or spaghetti we could make from my half of this windfall, for we needed all we could use, given the consumption of my perpetually hungry children—who could burn protein-rich calories like professional wrestlers.

No, it was the *other* smell that disturbed me. After I'd opened it—after I'd broken the hymen of pelt by punching the blade of my knife into the short, white hairs of the hindquarters, circumcised and loosened the sphincter (quite skillfully I might add), tied it off with a piece of kite string that I'd fished from the right breast pocket of my red-and-black-checked mackinaw, and then slit the belly "from breastbone to anus," spilling stomach and intestines and liver onto the leafy forest floor—I was overcome by the smell. A gagging, thick, steamy, bloody, sweet, acrid, *un*-deathlike smell rose into the darkening woods and attached itself like burdocks to my jacket and flannel shirt and moustache. It was un-deathlike because I knew the smell of death. I had been a union gravedigger at White Chapel Cemetery in Troy, Michigan, for two years prior to my pursuit of the Ph.D.; I had battled a mouse infestation in the walls of an old farmhouse with d-Con; I had jogged innumerable rural roads of Michigan, Ohio, and New York during early spring, when the ditches were riddled with rotting, thaw-exposed carcasses of possum, raccoon, deer, dog, cat, squirrel, and woodchuck.

But the stench that emanated from the body cavity of this obviously dead yet still life-warm animal was not like anything I'd ever smelled before.

It was more a smell of brown blood than red. It was rancid fat, not gristle. It was the smell of a Polish butcher shop on a muggy July day, mixed with the fragrances of the Omaha stockyards, a cheap pine car-freshener, and the smog that hazes I-94 around Gary, Indiana. It was iron smelt and sourdough yeast. It was a bathing suit left for days in a sour puddle on shaggy-carpeted floor. It was damp cement blocks and mold. It was soccer cleats and shin guards in the bottom of an athletic bag. Sulfur water and fungus. Ammonia. It was cob rot and corn husks and metal filings and sharp cheese. It was cabbage and petroleum. Diesel exhaust. The poopy diaper of a child who'd eaten creamed spinach . . .

There are really no words to describe it. It was, I think now, the smell of a creature in the process of becoming another kind of creature: the smell, say, of transmogrification through consumption. A *soul* taking the form of smell.

Or perhaps it was the smell of a heart enacting its own transformation—from a defender of life's beauty to its thief. The smell of responsibility and human selfishness. The smell of metamorphosis as it's theorized out of Darwinian evolution: the smell of predation and survival, the smell of dying.

SINCE THAT FIRST GUTTING, my knife has come to hold a significance for me that no other birthday gift ever has. It has never been the same. And I'm thankful that I didn't end up losing it that first day—at least not for very long.

After I'd successfully gutted the beast, I'd wiped my knife blade free of blood, hair, and tissue with a couple of yellow (still pliable) slippery elm leaves and then stabbed my knife into the ground so that I could use both hands to tie together the head and front legs of my stew meat with the length of rope I'd unbelted from my waist and thereby could more easily and safely drag it out to the road. In my anxious pride, not to mention my concern for the rapidly approaching darkness, I'd inadvertently left the knife embedded in the leaf rot and so had to return later with a flashlight to find it. After some harried moments of spooky meandering in the dark, I stumbled upon my scuffle marks from the gutting and was able to locate, just beyond the ripe entrails, my half-hidden knife. Fortunately,

I never had to confess to my children how careless I was with their thoughtful gift.

In the years following, the Camillus became a trusty companion as I kept us in meat by my practiced skill as a hunter. After each gutting, I'd carefully re-hone the knife to a razor-sharp edge (which eventually reduced the blade nearly to the point of its needing to be replaced.) The gift served me well—served us all, during our years in rural New York.

It was finding the knife behind the abandoned jock straps in my underwear drawer the other day that reminded me of my first gutting. I hadn't thought of it for years. Since we've moved back to Michigan, and a more lucrative position, one that provides me with money enough for pure Angus beef in sterile, sealed packages, I've only used the knife twice. Once for *sport* (or spite), I shot a tomato-foraging doe with a bow and arrow from my children's treehouse and used the knife to gut her. And then, years later, for my youngest son's ninth-grade biology project, we used the knife to dismantle a chicken and boil it down to bones, which Andrew then reassembled in skeleton form, using wire and a glue gun. In the second instance, while the blade had been sharp enough for groping through the feathers and flesh, I'd discovered that the spring mechanism which allows one to fold the blade had worn or broken in the intervening years, and so the knife no longer locked open with a satisfying click. It was no longer safe to use. At any moment the blade could fold unexpectedly and send one's finger to the emergency room in a sandwich bag. That's probably why I'd hid it away.

Yet, as I unsheathe it now and hold the knife in my hand, as I thumb off the green oxidation that dulls the nickel and brass ends, I can still smell that indescribable stench of my first gutting—its triumph and foolishness—and I'm convinced I can still see, in spite of three dozen washings or more, the black stain of first blood in the blade's hinge.

OCCUPATIONAL HAZARDS

When I decided in my junior year of high school that I wanted to be a writer, I knew my work was cut out for me. My academic preparation up to that moment had been less than remarkable, particularly as I had a certain knack for being removed from one class or another as a "disruptive influence." "To be a writer" would mean that I would have to "buckle down" (as my father would say) and to immerse myself in the literary tradition, which would most likely be accomplished by studying English at a college or university. I needed guidance, for one thing. For another, if my high school record was any indication—and I'm not talking about just grades here—I needed discipline. To that end, for the next decade or so I sought higher education like an addiction, going from one college to another, degree after degree, in pursuit of a writer's life. I injected myself with the drugs of choice for literary addicts: authors and texts, scholarship and methodology, rhetoric and workshop. And while over time I became a deliberate and conscientious academic—motivated in no small way by draft deferments—I was nonetheless naive when it came to thinking in practical terms, as in occupational endeavors. Only after the acquisition of a Ph.D. from Bowling Green State University, after eleven years of accumulating a literary foundation, was I forced (by impending family) to face the practicality of what my writer-wannabe addiction had driven me to become. That's when I turned to what I knew best—my graduate study having been supported with teaching fellowships—and sought a career in higher education.

Teaching helped to pay the bills on a regular basis. Something I'd not given much thought to for most of the 1970s, despite a subconscious knowledge that my Romantic (writerly) notions had all the sustenance of a Pet Rock. On the contrary, I was fully aware that a decision to pursue a writer's life would require not only economic adaptability—especially given the birth-order unlikelihood of any parental patronage—but a certain amount of suffering as well.

Both of which I was able to manage through an assortment of "odd" jobs. One summer I drove the kiddie train at the Clinch Park Zoo. Another I dipped ice cream at the House of Flavors. I life guarded and taught swimming. I worked in the quick freeze at Chef Pierre Pies, maneuvering wobbly carts of freshly made pastries across icy floors and then hauling out the frozen results for packaging. I spent the summer after receiving my bachelor's degree as a counselor and water polo coach at an uppity boys' camp in Maine (—and no, I didn't know anything about water polo at the time). That same fall, I pumped gas at the first 24-hour convenience store to open in Grand Traverse County (Holiday). Another summer I worked "maintenance" at the Star Pin Company in Shelton, Connecticut, a job which consisted primarily of reglazing factory windows four stories above a paving-stone alley. For the two-year lapse between my masters and Ph.D., I worked as a union gravedigger at White Chapel Cemetery, in Troy.

The jobs were for the most part more boring than difficult, often quite thankless, but I seldom minded, since they served a primary function: they helped sustain the body that housed my soon-to-be-educated mind and they allowed me to make car payments. Besides (I would at times remind myself) they were for the most part "temporary" and not life-threatening.

With one exception. In the summer of 1973, I drove a delivery truck for Seyfert's, a "snack rack" company (potato chips, pork rinds, pretzels). Based in Indiana, Seyfert's was the third-largest potato chip distributor in Northwest Lower Michigan.

My brother-in-law got me the job. He was the Route Supervisor. I don't recall what we drivers were actually titled, though I know it wasn't just "driver." We may have been Route Salespersons or Route Service Managers, or some such, as we were technically expected to do more than simply take orders and deliver chips. (Titles notwithstanding, in the bureaucratic hierarchy of the snack food industry, drivers were merely one step above the warehouse flunkies—those high school drop-outs who couldn't pass the commercial driver's license test.) Few of us that summer did any more than overload displays, since Made Rite, our biggest competitor, was on strike for most of June. We chip drivers had all we could do to fill Made Rite's vacant racks with bags of Seyfert's pretzels and popcorn.

My route included all of Leelanau and Benzie Counties, as well as the western half of Grand Traverse County, not counting Traverse City proper. The whole circuit took three long days, and so I made the complete route twice each week. If I hustled Thursday and Friday, I could finish on Saturday by late afternoon. More often, my typical day started about 5 a.m., when I would leave my parents' house in Lake Ann in order to get to the warehouse for loading about 5:30. I'd get back to Lake Ann about 10 p.m. The days were long, to be sure, but I was making more money than I'd ever made before, my "take home"—on straight commission—over $300 a week. Not bad for 1973. (Especially considering that the year before, at Holiday, I was making $1.10 an hour—a dime-an-hour more for night shift . . .)

Then, the last week of June, my good fortune nearly tanked. I had gotten an early start that Friday, and so by 9 a.m. I was well on my way up the eastern side of Leelanau County, already through Suttons Bay and headed for Northport. I made my normal stop at Rick's Marina and Bar at the top of the hill in Omena, and as the day was warming nicely—the sun a blinding sparkle on West Bay—I found myself shedding the light jacket I'd started the day with.

Omena General Store was my next stop. The store sits at the bottom of the hill below Omena, just before where M-22 takes a sharp left and heads away from West Bay. I pulled my truck onto the gravel turn-off at right side of the road, splashing up onto the manifold a couple of the puddles that had been formed from the night's rain. The truck knocked and coughed longer than usual when I shut it off (and not for the first time). I climbed from the cab, crossed the road, and entered the store, my order pad in hand. My routine was to fill out the pad and then leave the bill with the owner while I went out to the truck and brought in whatever cases of chips and snacks I'd need. That way, I wouldn't have to wait very long after I loaded the rack; payment (usually in the form of a check) would be ready when I was done.

I had only been in the store a minute or two, sizing up how much of Made Rite's space I could safely wrest from the Frito-Lay driver, when Bill, behind the counter, asked if that was my truck parked across the road.

"The red one?" I said.

"Yes."

"Yes, that'd be me."

"I think your truck's on fire," he said, leaning on the counter with what later seemed to me undue casualness.

"Probably just steam," I said, not even looking up from my corn chip count. "I splashed up a couple of the puddles when I stopped."

"I don't think so," he said. "I think it's on fire."

Sure enough, when I looked out, I could see that the smoke rising from the engine compartment was darker than it should have been if it had been steam. So I asked to use the store phone—more calmly than I imagined I would be in such circumstances, probably due in part to Bill's underwhelming acknowledgement—and I called the warehouse.

The boy that answered—P.J.—was the one employee that John, the owner of Northern Distributors, refused to give a route to. P.J. was actually some relative of John's wife, if I recall, but so irresponsible that he was simply assigned to "manage" the warehouse, helping drivers to load and unload.

"Is John there?" I said.

"Getting coffee," he said. "Is there a problem?"

"Could be," I said. "I think my truck's on fire."

"Whatdaya mean?" said P.J.

"I mean, my truck's on fire. I just wanted to know what John wanted me to do about it."

"Does it still run?" the boy asked. "Can you finish your route?"

"It's *on fire,*" I repeated. "Right now. I can see it burning. So I don't know if I can finish my route or not. Just leave John the message, okay?"

"Okay," he said. "Should I tell him where you are?"

"I'm at the Omena General Store," I said. "I'll go out and see how bad it is. I'll call back when I find out more."

By the time I'd gotten across the road, I could see an occasional flame lick the grill of the cab. The paint on the center of the hood had begun to blacken. It occurred to me that I should probably salvage anything of value, so I went around the back of the truck—well away from the fire—and to the passenger side door. The only things of value (to me) were my jacket, with my checkbook in the pocket, and a case of Pabst Blue Ribbon long-necks, which one of the beer drivers had given me in exchange for a couple wholesale cases of curly potato chips (for his family reunion) at a previous stop. After setting the case of beer and my jacket a safe distance away, I stood a few feet from the front of the truck and watched the windshield darken with smoke.

Bill yelled from the porch steps of the General Store to tell me he'd called the fire department. He also said I probably shouldn't stand too close. The paint in the middle of the hood was now bubbling and cracking; black smoke bellowed from all sides of the engine compartment.

Soon the Omena Volunteer Fire Department (OVFD)—which consisted entirely of Rick, from Rick's Marina—came waddling down the hill with a portable fire extinguisher in one hand, a kitchen mitt on the other. Gray-haired, red-faced, and carrying a good deal of excess weight, Rick did not exude much confidence (in my mind) of rescue capability or disaster resolution. But Rick, it seems, was all we had.

He greeted Bill by saying that he'd called Suttons Bay for back up. He then said that it looked like a gas or oil fire, which rendered the use of his kitchen extinguisher improbable. (As the bar's short order cook he knew this from experience.) He then decided to find out what exactly was burning, so he released the engine compartment latch with his kitchen-mitt-hand and popped the hood open.

The burst of oxygen shot flames ten feet into the air. And confirmed that the engine was indeed on fire—concentrated in the carburetor. The circular air filter looked like a pan on a gas burner turned up too high—flames enveloped it. I turned and looked down at the water of West Bay, which was barely twenty feet away, calm, and sparkling with morning sun. I said, "If we only had a bucket . . ."

Rick immediately denounced that idea, mumbling something about water on oil fires. He was at the same time reaching his kitchen-mitted hand into the inferno—more flame than smoke, now that the paint on the hood was no longer involved—and untwisting the wing nut that held down the air filter. Once he'd done that, he grabbed the whole works and flicked it like a flaming Frisbee into the water, where it sizzled briefly before sinking.

"Sand," he said.

The next thing I knew the two of us were grabbing handfuls of beach sand and throwing them into the carburetor. Sure enough, the fire was soon out.

Back in the store, Bill phoned Suttons Bay and cancelled the fire call; I phoned John (back from having coffee) and—pumped with a sudden frantic concern for my safety and future—quit. But John didn't buy it. He talked me down, and within an hour, P.J. had brought out the "spare" truck. We repacked the stock from the back of the Ford Inferno to the GMC—miraculously there had been no damage to the chips—and I continued on my route.

By then, I was about five hours behind.

Of course, no one had taken the time to explain to me why the spare truck was a "spare." While newer than the one I'd been driving, they both had about the same mileage. I assumed that the GMC was seldom used because the truck was one of the few manual transmissions left in the fleet; most of the drivers preferred automatics. I never thought to ask.

The half-day I'd lost to the fire meant I had to bypass the smaller customers on that day and push on to the major stores and bars, so they'd have chips for the weekend. So it wasn't until the following week that I got back to servicing the Platte River campgrounds and the Empire Coast Guard station. Fortunately, the spare truck seemed to run fine, though I was pushing it pretty hard, given that the next weekend was July Fourth. Everybody wanted their chip racks full, if not overflowing, for the holiday. The businesses I'd skipped the week before—like Miller's Canoe Rental—were especially vocal in making sure they'd not again be caught without Slim Jims and pork rinds.

So I was hustling, and, admittedly, more impatient than I should have been in servicing my route. I would be out of the cab before the truck even rocked to a stop, and back on the road nearly before the authorized signature on the business check was dry.

My pace was stalled at the Empire Coast Guard Station, one of the most time-consuming and least productive of my Leelanau County stops. I serviced the officer's club, the NCO Club, and the white radar dome at the top of the hill. At the dome, I would knock on a white door in the base, and then wait for some time before someone would crack open the door and buy four or six vending-sized brownies, a bag or two of sunflower seeds, and an occasional candy bar. The stop was ridiculous, in my estimation, as it took more time than most and generated very little in sales. But it was a stop I had to make nonetheless.

Because I was in a hurry and generally there is no traffic in the base, I simply stopped the truck in the road that ran beside the radar dome, shut it off but left it in gear, and decided to save time I'd simply take a boxful of assorted items up to the door. Angled downhill, the truck lurched forward slightly as I reached for the door handle, so I set the emergency brake. I sold two brownies, two bags of sunflower seeds, and a Snickers.

When I got back into the truck, it again lurched forward from the weight of my entry. I started the engine, and with my right foot on the regular brake, pressed down with my left foot the emergency brake in order to release it. There was an unsettling sound of a cable *snap*, then the emergency brake handle began to swing loosely. The next thing I knew, I was careening down the hill—no brakes, no transmission. I shut off the engine and let out the clutch. Nothing—except the loss of any power steering I might have had.

It was then that I decided—in an odd moment of calmness, sort of like movie slo-mo—that I should consider my options.

Ahead of me was an intersection, in the middle of which stood two uniformed service people in apparent conversation. Because it was coming up fast, the intersection itself did not provide me with any alternatives to my careening—even if I was able to somehow avoid plowing over the two people gabbing in the road—other than forcing the steering wheel to the left or right and lodging a potato chip truck in one of the barracks. Beyond the intersection, farther down the hill, was my only other opportunity—a T, where the road I was barreling down ended at a crossroad that ran along the ridge above Empire. I would have three choices there: I could try and swing the truck to the left and follow the road down the hill and into the village (which I immediately recognized as "stupid," since that was the same road the Grand Traverse Sports Car Club used in their annual hill climb rally); or I could leap out of the truck and let it—and three thousand dollars' worth of snack food—plunge through the small yellow wooden barrier and crash into the ravine below; or I could try and swing the truck to the right, which would propel it UP the slight incline in that direction and, with any luck, roll to a stop.

I chose the third.

It was like something out of a B movie. I was honking and waving, mashing down the brake pedal over and over, rocking the truck back and forth (expecting such motion to slow it down?). At first, the guys at the intersection waved back. Then they leapt out of the way and yelled about my speed as I went by. I made a wide turn, my tires screeching, the load tumbling in the back, both hands wrenching the steering wheel as I held on for dear life, the sound of shoulder gravel smattering the fender wells. And then it was over. I was stopped in front of the NCO Club. A trail of oil and grease marked my journey from the white dome.

The two guys I had managed not to kill in the first intersection ran up to see if I was okay. The dangling drive train, separated from the rear axle, had alerted them to the suggestion that something may have gone wrong. The manager in the NCO club then let me in the building to use the phone to call the warehouse—yet only after I'd been sure to take his chip order. Again, I called John. Again, I quit. Again, John sent out P.J with the OTHER spare truck, and together we salvaged what chips we could and continued the route.

I didn't go into work the next day. Every time John or my brother-in-law called, I quit again. But, sad-to say, I was back on the job by Friday. With the ride-along help of P.J., temporarily promoted from "warehouse kid," I was able to get caught up on the route before the weekend.

It was, after all, the Fourth of July, and how could *any* Michigander, let alone an out-of-state vacationer, celebrate that Great American Holiday without potato chips?

ONCE BITTEN

The dog came out of nowhere.

—An auspicious start, if I don't say so myself. For the sentence captures both the reader's attention and the immediacy of the moment when, as I was peddling my bike along 16 Mile Road northwest of Big Rapids, Michigan, a Collie-like mongrel bit me.

It was "out of nowhere" because I hadn't been expecting any challenge to my right-of-way as I passed the ancient farmhouse. I was looking ahead, to where the road humps over US 131 a mile north of Exit 139, and calculating whether or not I would need to downshift. I wasn't thinking of any danger. I'd ridden that route dozens of times and never had any prior encounter with vicious canines, never felt a need to intensify my vigilance, as I would while riding certain other roads of Mecosta County, roads that harbor threats in the guise of untethered, cyclist-chasing dogs. It is "out of nowhere" because, on another level (figuratively and formally), that's where the first sentence of any essay seems to come from—for the reader, at least—although it's a *nowhere* of some account, given its function as an introduction, meant to capture one's attention, establish interest, and/or set the tone of the story to follow.

That is to say, I'd not expected an attack, not expected the surprise of sudden *huffs* that came alongside just before the snap and growl, which seemed to occur simultaneously—not unlike the way my own dog would, as a puppy, both snarl and clutch some ratty, de-squeakered, half-stuffed dog toy (formally, say, a duck or a squirrel) as we played tug-of-war. Yet, now that I think about it, perhaps both hail and heed are not possible at the exact same time, for the Collie mix wasn't tugging. It had assailed me in a quick, fluid blitz. The growl may in fact have come first, shortly followed by the snap, or perhaps just after, as a kind of bully-show (*i.e., Should you violate my protectorate again, you're likely to get worse!*).

Whatever the case, my response was immediate.

"Hey!" I yelled. A loud, forceful scream is often enough to deter a dog attack, should one appear to be imminent (although, admittedly, not so effective after the fact). I braked to a stop, itself an action—like a counter threat—that in my previous experience had served to send undisciplined pets in retreat. Then, "Shit!" Though I could barely feel it, I could see my right ankle had begun to ooze blood.

The next thing I noticed was an elderly man standing in the unpaved drive, caught as if in a senior-moment between the wood-sided farmhouse (badly in need of paint) and an unattached garage-like outbuilding. Whether he'd actually witnessed the aggression or not, I don't know. But he was acting (in my mind) as if nothing of any consequence had happened, which fueled my sudden fury. An affront of disregard! I dismounted my bike and began wheeling it up the drive, favoring with a pronounced limp my bleeding ankle. "Your dog just bit me!" I yelled at him. "Your stupid dog just bit me! I need to call the police!"

IT'S AT THIS POINT OF THE NARRATIVE arc that we should pause and place the circumstances in perspective, not only so the reader will more readily comprehend the significance of these details, but also for expository pacing. Since we'd entered the story *in medias res*—"into the middle of things," a common literary and dramatic technique for generating interest (think of the TV series *CSI*)—it behooves us to sustain that interest by gentle intrusion—that is, suspending the forward action and filling in the blanks.

I'd been cycling earnestly for several years—ever since jogging in cheap sneakers caused (so I was told) an extremely painful plantar fasciitis in the heel of my right foot. To be clear, I'd begun biking *again*, after years of jogging (which I'd taken up for its short-time, high-calorie burn), since foot pressure on a pedal did not aggravate the fasciitis in the way that a couple hundred pounds hammering upon size-eight athletic shoes did. Not only that, I enjoyed it; I found myself looking forward to my daily rides, which sometimes stretched for hours. Time was no longer an issue. The last of my four parental responsibilities was away at college, leaving my classes at Ferris State University the only schedule I had to accommodate. Besides, I found biking to be far superior to slogging a middle-aged body nine times around a 1/3 mile cul-de-sac; I liked the idea that I was *going* somewhere, and going there fast. I took to bicycling with a passion—an obsession, perhaps—riding six days a week (during Michigan's biking "season," April to November) and averaging between twenty and thirty miles a day.

"And you've only been bitten twice!" Cindy exclaimed, later. "That's remarkable. You've been pretty lucky overall."

Nor could I disagree. However, I was divorced at the time of the Collie bite, and not involved with anyone, so my conversation with Cindy, repeated here, is intended to enhance characterization rather than to further plot or background, fleshing out the narrator (so to speak), by making him believable, and personable—even empathetic—through the staging of some reasonable interaction with a partner. (*Unusual circumstances*, the reader is meant to think. *He's not such a bad guy* [especially considering what is about to take place at the farmhouse on 16 Mile Road].) The truth is, Cindy's comment may merely represent what I *imagined* a person named Cindy might say, a person whom I may have been involved with (briefly) after the incident and who therefore could verify its legitimacy (although anyone familiar with me, or my relationships, would already assume that legitimacy, based on the factuality of Cindy's existence).

And yet. Truth being what it is—truth being *truth*—there is no real need for me to distinguish the actual from the embellished in this instance, except as a way to authorize this particular document as nonfiction (which the parenthetical concerning expository craft—above—already seems to do.)

THE FIRST TIME I WAS BITTEN had been more than twenty years before, in the Finger Lakes of Upstate New York, the first year I taught at Keuka College. At that time, my wife Debbie and I were renting the lower part of a house owned by the president of the college, about two miles from campus. We were expecting our first child and had only one car, so I often biked to class. One day, as I was riding my red Fuji Sport 10 on the lower road that ran beside Keuka Lake, a Doberman popped out from between two cars parked along the shoulder and ripped off a chunk of my sweatpants (left leg). Fortunately, he'd not gotten any skin. (Full disclosure: I am assuming it was a *he*; I didn't stop to verify.)

Did I mention that both incidents occurred in October? A time of year in which, studies show, there is an increase in aggression among predatory creatures? That hormones can get cranky in changeable weather? That I may have startled a wolf-cousin out of a lazy autumnal nap? Or did each dog perhaps feel threatened by my unleveled breathing—my chuffing—and *whish* of tire—and hum of bike chain—enough to attack?

Then again, perhaps October had nothing to do with it. I can't really substantiate any coincidence in terms of the separate aggressions. All I know for sure is that the very coolness of morning may have saved me from harm in the first instance, as I had dressed appropriately in warm sweatpants; in the second, a glorious spate of Indian Summer meant I was still wearing shorts.

THE COLLIE MIX—and the reader must now recognize, of course, we're back in the thick of things, having provided both history and reflection in the prior paragraphs, in preparation for what will take place. While the paragraph break alone may have been enough transition for a perceptive reader, the repetition of the "Collie mix" is helpful in re-situating us in present time, in the central plot, that of the *second* bite, for I had identified the first bite, you will recall, as that of a Doberman (first in chronology, not narrative).

Picture me wheeling my bike up the scrappy driveway of a small, weathered farmhouse on 16 Mile. By the time I reach him, the dog is cowering behind the elderly man, who is wearing, in addition to what might be considered typical farmer's denim work clothes, an apologetic, even frightened, look on his worn, scraggly face. Upon my closer examination, the dog hardly seems capable of—or desirous of—harming anyone, and I suddenly begin to wonder if I am making a mistake. Can animals be blamed for acting like animals?

Still, adrenaline propels me forward.

"Your dog bit me," I growled, and I turned my ankle for the man to see. The wound was bleeding profusely—no doubt exacerbated by the exhilaration of physical exercise. A four-inch trail of blood had reached my low-cut athletic socks. It looked horrible, much worse than I knew it was. Still, I was thinking *rabies*. I was thinking *shock*. And pet owner liability. And property insurance . . .

"I'd like to use your phone to report it," I said.

THE OLD GUY ASKED ME if I would mind waiting a minute, so he could alert his wife that I would be coming in. Then he beckoned to me and held the door. Beyond a mudroom cluttered with boots and shoes, coats, hats, and a variety of work gloves, I entered a small, dark kitchen. A wall phone hung just inside the door. I talked to Animal Control first—the dog-owner had dialed the number for me and had given the deputy, whom he seemed to know on a first-name basis, the address. Then I called my son Matthew, who was living in Big Rapids at the time, having graduated from Hope College; he worked for the Mecosta County EMS. (Yes, the very same "child" we were expecting at the time of my first dog bite.) I thought that if Matthew was available he could pick me up and transport me to the hospital (more for an official report than for the injury). But when I couldn't reach him, I simply rode my bike the six or seven miles back to my house and then drove myself to the ER, where the wound was cleaned and bandaged and the police again took my information. I received a tetanus shot.

I found out later that the dog had had an earlier incident with a bicyclist; it was not rabid, just old, maybe half-blind; the couple's home insurance would cover any medical costs; and if I agreed not to sue them in the future, I would receive $200 as a good faith settlement.

I'm skipping ahead, of course. The reader is surely aware by now that the narrative is not about the dog bite at all—since very little has come of it, really, the trauma overplayed (in both my mind at the time and in retrospect). Especially given the number of interjections along the way, which are often used to slow the reader's progress and/or imply that something else is involved, some analogous connection that will, eventually, render meaning. (Maybe something that the writer is avoiding, circling the topic instead of approaching it head on; snapping at it, so to speak, in opposition to one's firm grasp and tug . . .). Notice how I've over stressed the details in parentheses—details that occur outside of the incident itself—which also could be construed either as a method for building up anticipation or for rendering believability through specificity (which I don't mean to challenge here—the story is quite true). Still, I haven't yet given as much attention to what I'd encountered inside that small and shabby farmhouse as I'd made those calls. The perceptive reader—if persisting this far—would surely recognize that lapse as an intentional one, as a device of exposition.

Everything in the house was *old*: from the black wall phone with the over-stretched cord (receiver smelling of unbrushed teeth and pork sausage), to the gray and yellow Formica kitchen table, the matching aluminum-framed vinyl-padded chairs (an occasional rip held closed with Scotch tape), to the countertop and sink piled with Mason jars and breakfast dishes, to the ancient, round-shouldered refrigerator, the metallic handle dull with use . . .

The couple themselves were old. The dog—now lying meekly on a scatter rug near the door—looked old. The house smelled old, the way long-inhabited and overheated houses smell. Even the couple's gestures and apologies—their respectful offers of coffee, water, bandages, a ride to the hospital—their concerns—were *old*.

And unexpected.

At the table sat the woman's mother, her shoulders draped with a ratty housedress. She must have been ninety or more, kind of half-smiling, absently, as if in feeble greeting of a guest she didn't recognize, unaware—I would guess—of the small miseries I was about to impose on these well-meaning people, the family dog that would be removed from their care . . .

I nearly gave in, when I saw her. I nearly choked out "Sorry" and retreated, for it was likely that this elderly farm couple, in their poverty, were doing all they could for the mother, likely that their poverty itself was the reason she was sitting there. It was something that I was familiar with. I had spent months in similar circumstances—coping as best as I could while I cared for my parents during their decline and deaths (my father in June, my mother in October of the year before, *to the day*).

But I didn't give in. I carried forth, boldly and blindly. As the reader already knows.

I never learned the dog's name. I never even asked.

BETWEEN KENNEL AND CREEK

1.

We are not likely of a single mind as we celebrate the sun's sour breath the last week of March, a patently dreary month this year, remarkable for how often the meteorologists of West Michigan updated the record number of overcast days in "recorded history." It's the lead story on many channels—trumping any regional concern for political piracy, gender dysphoria, or the looming extirpation of several species (bipeds among them)—and consequently has stirred me into action. I've taken to the yard, where I can distance myself from the media's daft diversions by virtue of some mindless repetitive task (which generally promotes, in my case, emotional composure and contemplation). Consider the term *recorded history* itself. On the one hand, it is an anthropocentric misnomer, representing as *historical* our culture's madcap fascination with superlative aberrancies in climactic observation; on the other, it is mere tautology: the word *history* defined in my *American Heritage Dictionary* as "a chronological *record* of events" [my italics].

WOOD TV, the NBC-affiliated television station in Grand Rapids, refers to its weather department as *Storm*

Team 8; WWMT, the CBS affiliate licensed in Kalamazoo, promotes the forecasting segment of its daily news broadcast as generated by *The Severe Weather Center*. Neither station appears to have any interest in the calm between storms, nor in any manifestation of weather considered *normal, usual,* or *average*. Consequently, they no longer serve my interest in observing the unremarkable calm of this cloudless, early spring day.

2.

WHILE A CONSIDERABLE AMOUNT of research has provided evidence that the Sun Dance was a predominant tribal ceremony of Great Plains Indians, anthropologists are less certain as to whether a similar tradition was practiced by the indigenous tribes of the Great Lakes region. Beyond the reputed burial and ceremonial mounds of certain Paleo-Indians discovered in Southwest Lower Michigan, "evidence of these ancient cultures is meager," admits the posted research from the Department of Geography at Michigan State University. The earliest regional tribes of record—the Chippewa, the Ottawa, and the Potawatomi—were thought to be primarily agricultural. Their sustenance depended as much on rain as sun. Thus their predominant tribal celebrations took place during, or immediately after, harvest.

There is no evidence that indigenous peoples of Michigan—whose history can be traced back approximately 10,000 years—found any interest in tracking and then establishing a *record* for the consecutive number of sunless days. A suddenly cloudless day in spring was likely no cause for celebration, sour or otherwise.

3.

TODAY WILL BE *MOSTLY SUNNY*, they say. And this morning, by my way of thinking, *sour and warm*. Warmth begat by sourness, I'm guessing, as the thaw has released into the suddenly still air winter's moisture and from that moisture winterkill's pent-up scents: compost and decay, odorously reminiscent of the memorial grounds in Southeast Lower Michigan where I'd worked as a gravedigger some fifty years before.

THE PASTURE HAS BEEN FREED, mostly, of the layer of ice left behind by last week's late-season storm, a storm that also amputated—imprecisely (as by shoddy application of an osteotome)—the ancient pine that once stood handsomely between our house and barn like a monument to an earlier time, a time before houses and barns. Now, post-storm, the pine is not so grand; to the contrary, its bark-less and shattered limbs raise some concern for the safety of any horses paddocked below, which gives me pause (wherein I estimate the cost and timing of the tree's safe removal).

The significantly younger red maples beyond the barn have, in contrast, begun to affirm their names in the burgundy blush of twig-tips and buds—despite several days of wind-chills in the teens—and the newsworthy sun—*finally!*—is nudging the more slumberous sugar maples along the road, stirring their sweet promise.

Odd, I think, the lack of bird-call on such a morning. Do I intimidate? Initially, the only sound is the whoosh and snap of the pine boughs I've been loosing from their scattered disarray and piling beside the chipper. Until I no longer can. For the larger, most ground-level of the fallen limbs are imbedded in what stubborn ice remains beneath the loose, sun-drawn dark-needled smaller branches I've separated for the burn pile. Well-shaded below the pine, and under winter's record-breaking overcast, the ice has trapped some of the lowest branches in its slow withdrawal, mimicking in microcosm—as in a museum diorama—the glacial retreat of Michigan's mile-high maker some 11,000 years ago.

ADDING TO THE OTHERWISE songless air the grunt of human effort.

4.

ANCIENT, IN DESCRIBING THE PINE, is a relative term, for the tree is no record-breaker, in terms of tree-longevity, nor even in measure of human duration. ("One of the oldest trees on earth, a spruce in Sweden," writes Tim Flannery, in the Foreword to Peter Wohlleben's *The Hidden Life of Trees*, "is more than 9,500 years old.") Yet the sheer size of the pine beside the paddock, the one whose fallen branches I have been troubling to unearth, suggests that it has surely outlived my parents and possibly my grandparents. It's even possible that my great-grandfather, who—at the turn of the century more than a century ago—lived on a dairy farm within stalking distance of this very tree, may have in fact stood beneath it for shelter during a sudden snow squall while out hunting for deer or small game (or a lost calf). It is a long-standing tree—as evidenced by its increasing infirmity, its routine deadfall—and I could have simply called it *old*.

Yet in the quiet of this morning—an unnatural quiet, it seems to me, as I am the only sound apparent—*old* doesn't cut it (if you excuse the pun). *Old* is the sound of the locomotive that howls from the bottom of the next hill when the wind is right, as it tracks beside the Grand River on its way to deliver chemicals to Amway's production facility in Ada. *Old* is the sound of the great horned owl that occasionally sentinels in the dead sassafras at the edge of our property line (and not its more vocal barred cousin, whose call has the anxious tone of a lovesick pubescent boy).

"I REJOICE THAT THERE ARE OWLS," exclaims Thoreau, in *Walden*. "Let them do the idiotic and maniacal hooting for men. It is a sound admirably suited to swamps and twilight woods which no day illustrates, suggesting a vast and undeveloped nature which men have not recognized."

Old is the sound of a soft, dry pine log split by hand—when the maul thunks the stump.

Ancient, on the other hand, is something entirely different. Something tarnished, yet transcendent. It is the sound of a moon upon which humans have stood and explored, have technologically (and astronomically) dispatched, and yet remains to our earthbound sleepless human observation nothing very different from that of more ancient peoples of earth—or aliens, if one is inclined to believe. *Ancient* is sound that has been displaced, the way quiet displaces morning—which I would normally (and thoughtlessly) have already disrupted with my garrulous wood chipper. *Ancient* is not simply older old; it is more the sound of old. It is not the reappearance of sun but the faint explosive roil of sunburst on the surface of a star that eight-and-one-half minutes ago, give or take, produced the light (and warmth) that allows me to consider the inhuman quiet of a morning as metaphoric and meaningful.

5.

ALSO ODD THAT NONE OF MY neighbor's squat-jowled bulldog pups sniff and huff at the chain-linked kennel to the west of our fence line. None bark at my dim shape moving through the unexplored realm of their imagination, which at other times likely populates with dangerous, uncanine-like monsters or feline irritants worth railing at. No thrum of machinery disturbs them—not even from beyond the kennel and down Timpson Road a ways, where a new house is rising stank-angled and plastic from a hole excavated out of a dozed "clearing"—that is, where woods somewhat older than our red maples but younger than our pine had just weeks before entangled a small hill—and which now elevates the western horizon to a point that reduces the last glimmer of sun at certain times of year by one or two minutes.

Nor has Bryan, our neighbor to the east, yet to rise and address the damage the storm has dumped on his front walk like a winter's worth of weekly advertising supplements—vestiges of the uprooted maple he will chainsaw into firewood and haul in his rickety trailer (behind a mufflerless ORV) to whomever down the way has not upgraded their fireplace to gas.

6.

"BUT THEIR DOGS, WHERE ARE THEY?" Thoreau queries, in the "Sounds" chapter of his famous book, during a meditation on the "bleating of calves and sheep, the hustling of oxen," which he hears from a passing train, whose whistle mimics the shepherd's bell. He suspects the animals on the train are on their way to slaughter and so conjectures a rhetorical answer: "[The dogs] will not be in at the death.

. . . They will slink back to their kennels in disgrace, or perchance run wild and strike a league with the wolf and the fox."

THE FITCHBURG RAILROAD, which passes Walden Pond about a "hundred rods south" of Thoreau's cabin, takes up much of the author's contemplation in the chapter titled "Sounds." Trains are but one example of *commerce*, a concept hinged in Thoreau's mind so as to swing both literally and figuratively, as both boon and bane. Much is made of commerce in the chapter, the way it serves our human needs, in deference to our nature. He considers how the train that passes a hundred rods to the south of his cabin adds its voice to the "wilderness" with such quotidian regularity that farmers and woodsmen can set their clocks by it, and which appropriates not merely the calls of nature but of man's association to it.

"So is your pastoral life whirled past and away," he concludes.

7.

ALTHOUGH THE FIRST PATENT for what we now call a *chainsaw* was issued to Samuel J. Bens of San Francisco in 1905, it was only after World War II that developments in small engine design and the use of lightweight materials (notably aluminum) provided for the tool's deafening ubiquity. In North America, it was Robert Paxton McCulloch, founder of the McCulloch Motors Company, a manufacturer of small two-stroke gasoline engines, who in 1949 "revolutionized the chain saw industry by introducing a light one-man chain saw" (mcculloch.com). Since then, by virtue of marketing and DIY consumerism—not to mention various corporate acquisitions, merges, bankruptcies, and divisional sales (which include such iconic names as Black+Decker, MTD, and Husqvarna)—the McCulloch company has helped to raise the white noise level of "nature" by several decibels, adding to the sound of chainsaws an often-constant and ingratiating whine from lawnmowers, hedge trimmers, leaf blowers, garden tractors, generators, and other indispensable power equipment.

The commerce of medical science we call audiology, with its tangential plastic industries (i.e., the manufacture of sound suppression devices and/or hearing aids) might as well be credited to the development of the two-stroke engine.

8.

NOR HAS ANY BLUE JAY yet squawked awake this morning, nor cardinal begin its redundant alarm, nor carpool of crows roused themselves like morning traffic.

9.

ANCIENT, THEN, AND *UNWORLDY*—as if the earth is not yet the place of our disturbance.

Alas! Have we come to adore our noise so much that we are often uncomfortable in its absence, as if *unworldly* is itself defined by anthropogenesis? In considering the sound of the locomotive—which I called *old*—and acknowledging in this quiet its want, am I not also acknowledging the existential inevitability of trains, the well-documented boon and bane of railroads in the expansion and settlement of the American "frontier," not to mention its displacement of indigenous cultures and, somewhat more personally and allegorically, the unnatural quiet of this particular morning?

10.

MY FATHER AND I ARE ON our way to the county dump. It's the mid-1980s, a couple years before the barge called the Mobro 4000, loaded with 3,000 tons of New York City trash, gets turned away from its intended destination in North Carolina, and for five months floats off the Atlantic seaboard, drawing attention to the country's need to address a catastrophic waste disposal problem. ("Refuse Refused"—I recall thinking at the time—would make a clever headline for a news article about the incident, if not a good title for a poem, and I likely scribbled it on a piece of paper for later use. Much later I likely discarded it, thinking that surely someone else had already had the same idea—someone more literally demonstrative, more writerly. Perhaps, in fact, I had seen or heard "Refuse Refused" somewhere and thought the play on words so obvious as to be readily [and inevitably] appropriated. I can no longer be sure. At the time of the Mobro incident, my burgeoning family was barely managing to get by on the single salary I earned as an untenured assistant professor at a small struggling women's college. I seldom had opportunity to read the news, or much of anything beyond student papers or the nutritional statements on cereal boxes.)

We have loaded the "way back" of my father's Town & Country station wagon with an assortment of old, unsalvageable and unwanted items that had been abandoned—more likely discarded—in the clapboard farmhouse my older brother had purchased and was "renting" to my parents after they'd decided to move to Penn Yan, New York, where my wife and I and our three children—the youngest of their grandchildren—were living at the time. The two older of my children ride in the middle seat, having lobbied their easily swayed grandfather to go along—*A grand adventure! A trip to the dump!* We'd buckled them in as best we could without hassling to move their car seats from the cramped and tangled anchorage in the back of our second-hand family sedan. (Child restraints had become law in New York State in 1982, but we lived in rural, sparsely-populated Yates County and were "*only* going to the dump" . . .).

I don't recall what the garbage consisted of exactly—maybe old linoleum or cans of paint or plaster and lath or buckets of wallpaper paste—but it was stuff the regular garbage pick-up and county landfill would not accept. Consequently, my father and I had to haul it ourselves to a private facility on the other side of the county, which required that we drive around the end of Keuka Lake and across several sets of railroad tracks. As luck would have it, we had to stop for a train, the kids' first.

Consider our four different responses to this experience. Matthew, at five years old, is ecstatic: he's wide-eyed, squirming to see, yelling "Train! Train! Train!" to the dismay of Rachel, who, at three, is barely able to see much more than the tops of a few of the taller box cars from her deep-seated and tightly-belted position and so immediately begins to cry, frantically and unreasonably, causing her grandfather and me to wonder at first if she'd somehow gotten injured in the attempt. But no. Her screaming and carrying-on (we ascertained) were all because her brother could see something she couldn't. In an attempt at appeasement, I tried to distract her from her anguish by recounting how when my brothers and I were younger—not much older than she was—railroad crossings were so common that passing trains were treated more as a game than a cursed delay. We'd try to count the number of cars, or call out the different types, or guess where the auto-carriers were headed, or watch for the caboose. And, of course, wave at the conductor . . .

But since there was no way for Rachel to see a caboose—let alone a conductor—I just seemed to be making matters worse.

Then my father tried. Generally taciturn by nature, yet motivated in part to placate his teary granddaughter, he launched into his own story of trains, a story I had heard practically as many times as I'd been stopped at railroad crossings as a child riding in my father's car, waiting for the trains to pass. It went something like this:

> *During the war, my first command as a newly promoted captain was as the senior officer on a troop train traveling from boot camp in Arkansas to Florida, where we were supposed to catch a ride to England on some Navy transports. I was naive, as an officer, having gotten my commission by taking ROTC in high school and then at Michigan State and so when we stopped one night in some small town in Georgia, where we were to meet up with a train from the north, I was pretty liberal in handing out twelve-hour passes—any soldier who asked for one got one. After all, these poor kids had been cramped up pretty good for several days in the third-class cars, while we officers had some nice digs—we'd been assigned to someone's private coach, all brass fixtures and red velvet and personal waiters . . . It wasn't until the next morning that I'd realized my mistake. As our cars were being coupled to a larger train, its colonel, my commanding officer, asked us to muster the troops for roll call, to be sure no one had gone AWOL in the*

night. Apparently that was common problem with draftees. Fortunately, every one of my unit was accounted for. It was nothing short of a miracle.

My father loved trains. He often claimed to miss them (and not in the way one might, idiomatically, "miss the bus"). He missed the spit-shine and whistle of trains, the distant call of travel, the thrill of visiting new (and foreign) places. But by the mid 1980s, particularly in the more rural areas of Michigan or New York, where my father chose to live, passenger trains had nearly gone the way of the passenger pigeon. They were relics of another time and place, often operating on private stretches of abandoned tracks as tourist experiences (dinner trains and sightseeing tours), soon to be almost entirely transplanted by air freight and interstate "trucking," which itself would morph a decade later into "logistics."

To me, it was the same old story. But to my children, my father's story of the train, as he told it to his grandkids on the way to the dump—a story of soldiers off to war, of human oversight, of naiveté and salvation—was not so much an *old* story as an *ancient* one. A story of tarnished brass.

11.

ETYMOLOGICALLY, *WISDOM* HAS ATTACHED itself to *ancient* in the way certain well-cared-for automobiles or well-loved songs from our youth are considered "classic." *Ancient*, phonetically, may even tilt more toward *sagacious* than *elderly*. More *collectables* than *yard sale*. More *Packard Touring* than *jalopy*.

12.

I AM SORTING THROUGH the windfall beneath my ancient pine tree, separating what might be recycled—as logs for the fireplace, or chips for the garden path—from what is mere branch scrap and would be burned. The morning is, as I said, unnaturally and noticeably quiet, calm, reflective. Then the air—suddenly, for the first time this season, despite the stubborn ice beneath the deadfall—rises to a particular ambient temperature, at which the peepers from the creek near the road emerge from wherever mud or undergrowth they have been hibernating in and begin to fill the air with a trill so surprising and familiar as to be astonishing, drawing me out of my reminiscence and back into the present world, a world of noise and resurrection and affirmation.

13.

THE *PSEUDACRIS CRUCIFER*, more commonly known as the Northern Spring Peeper (or "chorus frog" or "false Acris") is named for the distinguishing X-shaped mark on its back, which resembles a crucifix. A group of peepers, according to *A Compendium of Collective Nouns*, would be called an *army*, "not because they're green like military fatigues," but more likely due to a biblical reference concerning Pharaoh's soldiers being routed by an army of frogs. Less frequently, a group of frogs is known as a "knot," which makes a good deal of sense to me, as I once exposed a small "knot" of tree frogs—a warmth-seeking cluster of clammy bodies—from behind the loose mortar of a chimney I was cleaning. But in describing the noise of spring peepers on this first warm day of spring, I'd tilt toward *army* as the collective noun—for I can picture a unit of the National Guard, each wielding a chainsaw, in a collective effort to clear a fire break down near the creek.

Yet given the reverberation of a community of sexually charged *Pseudacris*, perhaps an *engine* of frogs might be more metaphorically *à propos*.

It is spring, after all. The season of crucifer and crucifix—despite the late season's intolerance, the record-breaking cold and gray. *Let the stones of sleep be rolled aside*, sing the frogs. *Let the grave and the glorious be heard!*

Gentlemen, start your engines!

14.

IN THE PECKING ORDER OF HUMAN SENSES, our ability to hear is vastly overshadowed by our ability to see. Even our language reflects it: *overshadowed* a metaphoric sight word. Hearing, in fact, may be the least demonstrative and most easily manipulated of our senses, as attributed by people's (particularly married couples') stereotypical and often comical tendency for selectivity—that is, choosing what we want to hear (or hearing only what we choose). Unlike our vision, which tends toward perspective and interpretation, our hearing defaults to background noise. In fact, certain creatures of ancient evolutionary development—like snails—never "saw" a need for anything like ears. They sense their environment in other, more tactile, ways: through inaudible vibration.

Or honeybees, for that matter—with their preternatural ability to distinguish and remember scents or to perceive ultraviolet bands of color or to engineer mathematically perfect hexagonal structures in complete darkness—they have forgone the evolutionary need to hear.

15.

WOULD WE CALL THE SOUNDS *the world made before us / music?* asks the narrator of my poem "One Speaks of Loss," which I'd composed in the early 1980s, in partial meditation on the question of whether a falling tree in an unpeopled forest makes any noise. (A moot question, of course, as sounds, to humans, are mere sensory recognition of air "waves" or vibration, which a falling tree surely generates. The question, ultimately, is not one of sound but of our awareness.) The "loss" spoken of in the poem is that of a friend's father, who has suddenly (and unaccountably) disappeared—and not for the first time.

"One Speaks of Loss" is a poem—like much poetry—meant to give voice to the voiceless (or sound to its absence). What is the assumption of literature, save for that?

"All sound heard at the greatest possible distance," writes Thoreau, "produces one and the same effect, a vibration of the universal lyre, just as the intervening atmosphere makes a distant ridge of earth interesting to our eyes by the azure that it imparts to it." (The inexplicable, then, rephrased in terms of linguistic familiarity: a visual metaphor.)

And yet: "There came to me in this case a melody which the air had strained, and which had conversed with every leaf and needle of the wood, that portion of the sound which the elements had taken up and modulated and echoed from vale to vale. The echo is, to some extent, an original sound, and therein is the magic and charm of it."

Here on the ground before me lay the deadfall limbs of an ancient echo. Here, in the space between my neighbor's kennel and the small creek where spring peepers have begun to venerate the warmth of the sun. Here, the magic of regeneration; here, the charm of language and wilderness.

Given my age and the repetitive advice of my doctor, I will squeeze small rubber mutes into my ears to muffle—but not eliminate—the sounds of the frogs, not to mention the harmful grinding noise of my woodchipper. Only after that will I attend to the task at hand: the caretaking of the property I occupy and claim to own.

IV.

It's not coincidence that poets define their lives in terms of physical objects, especially those that manifest familiar metaphorical qualities.

A LESSON IN GEOGRAPHY

The hand is a lesson in geography" claims the speaker in my poem "A Widower Tells Other Passengers Where He's From." He's from Michigan, and so in response to the typical follow-up question ("*Where* in Michigan?"), I picture him flattening his right hand against the thin membrane of his personal space, fingers together but thumb slightly extended—like a kitchen mitt—the gesture that's second nature to all native Michiganders who travel beyond the Great Lakes. "*Here*," he'd say, stabbing with his left-hand index finger approximately where his hometown is located on the palm of his upraised right hand, the anatomic metaphor of our state's topography.

"Or the backside/ of the left," the poem continues, "forested with pine-like/ follicles along knuckled hills and shore-/ line, veined with purple interstates . . ."

I imagine he's a retired farmer, who has somewhat reluctantly begun to travel at the behest of his wife, recently deceased. Traveling was something he'd always promised her they'd do, eventually, though they'd neglected to take the time from the seasonal demands of his occupation, or in the healthful years of his wife's home economics, household management, and mothering. Then, when she grew older, and ill, he'd promised they'd travel when she got better. But it never happened. Now he joins third-ager tour groups visiting the most foreign places—those not likely haunted by the ghostly memories of a homestead and life together; he travels out of loneliness and guilt. Out of grief. And it's at one particular instance of his geographic identification of *home*—demonstrating to a cluster of college alumni on a cruise ship in the Mediterranean, say, or to an American couple he encounters among a wash of pigeons at Piazza San Marco—that he considers his hand more objectively:

Notice in particular the extremities:
thumb callused by the hard-held farm, blunt
and bruise-ruddied as a sugar beet; or
the wounds and healings, the jagged scars
our lumbered dunes have scoured.

In the academic year of 1992-93, when I taught as a Fulbright Lecturer at the University of Liège, Belgium, I'd found myself repeatedly locating my "hometown," of Big Rapids on the palm of my right hand—just so. In one instance, I meant to promote topographical awareness to my third-year American civilization students; in another, the gesture satisfied the curiosity of suburban Waterloo expatriates who were hosting a Fulbright reception. More often, mapping my hometown on my hand was simply a way of pandering to the casually intimate, friendly-face-in-a-foreign-crowd tourist we'd encounter during our continental meanderings. It was a gesture of second nature to me, a native Michigander (a term, by the way, despite its politically incorrect goosey-ness, I continue to prefer to the more current *Michiganian*), who had engendered the "handy" visual aid during multiple orientation ice-breakers at various colleges within the United States—a practice that most Americans could not imitate. For the Nebraska and Kansas classmates I'd met one year at Hastings College, for example, or the Kentucky and Georgia natives I'd studied with for my three years at Centre, or the Buckeye-bred Ohioans at Bowling Green State University, there was no part of the body one could use to point out the location of Americus or Grand Island or Bellevue.

The fact is, every time I trace the map of my right hand, I am more astonished by how my anatomy duplicates the expansive waterways and landforms of sand and copper-rich rock that were left in the retreat of the last local glacier, which gave up what we now call Michigan about 11,000 years ago.

If I cup my right hand loosely under a small stream of rainwater, the runoff will follow my lifeline east to west, the route of the Muskegon River, until it empties off the shore of my palm, where Lake Michigan should be. A crease below that one leads *west* to *east* along the path of the Chippewa River and into the Saginaw, which feeds the bay I've created with a space between my thumb and forefinger. Back across the state and slightly north, at the base of my little finger, there is a Platte-Lake-sized gap between the fleshy pads of that small digit and my ring finger, and I can easily make out the Platte River as it wends its way past the Water Wheel grocery store and Miller's Canoe Livery and along Benzie State Park to its mouth, which, during spring thaw and smelt-dipping, would be raucous with wader-splash, lantern-hiss, net-slap, and curses . . .

(I'm projecting backwards in time, now, as well as westerly, for the development of the Sleeping Bear National Lakeshore in the 1970s caused Miller's and the Water Wheel to be federally appropriated and summarily closed, leaving as the sole tourist enterprise the Park Service-monitored, seasonally-leased Riverside Canoe and Tube Rental. The former primitive-sites-only Benzie State Park has been transformed into a national campground, with RV hook-ups. And the smelt population—reduced in large part by the introduction of Coho salmon as a way to curb alewives—has yet to recover.)

Just there, on the outside of my palm, below where the dunes hunch like a sleeping bear, somewhere south of Empire, I have an inch-long scar that I acquired from the time we lived at a cottage on Platte Lake. It is one of several, in fact. Another, a small, whitish, lumpy nub, which may still harbor a fragment of storm window glass, pegs Lansing just east of the center of my grasp. To the north, Mackinaw City is an obvious smudge on police blotters—a thickly sliced heal-over on my middle finger. A lengthy, narrower scar runs down along the Lake Huron shore of my index finger like a Circle Tour Highway, while a crimp of skin the size and shape of I-275 circumnavigates where greater Detroit would be, in the southeastern corner of my palm's heel. And even below the wrist of my state line, a fat bulge of hairless flesh rises like a surprise of white hills somewhere along the Indiana-Illinois border, halfway between Indianapolis and Champaign.

Many of these landmarks (or should I say *hand*marks) are the consequence of adolescent recklessness—youthful rural sporting in the days before cable TV, slot cars, or eight-track tapes (let alone videos, Nintendo, or cell phones). They are memorable in the way punishment is, especially when one is punished for a wrong he didn't commit. Like the day I shoved my hand through the glass of a storm door.

As with most trauma, the details of what led to that incident are less clear than those of the aftermath, yet I've always felt family dynamics and birth-order are partially to blame. While my brothers and sisters and I totaled six, the father-off-to-war gap between Margaret and Richard (third and fourth child respectively) had created a situation where we were, for all practical purposes, two families—three older siblings and three younger. In that respect, I was not only fifth of six, but the middle child of the second wave—three boys: Richard (older) and Kenny (younger) on either side of me—and a half-generation younger than my sister Judy, the middle child of the first wave. By the time we'd moved to Platte Lake in the early 1960s, my oldest brother Robert was already married and serving the Army overseas, Judy was attending Kalamazoo College, and Margaret was in high school. During my formative years, except for summers and holidays, we "children" were pretty much just "the three boys"—and often referred to as such.

As such, we were a handful. I wouldn't necessarily call us "wild"—not like the three delinquent Sullivan boys up the road (whom we pretty much tried to avoid, except for Cub Scout meetings, and that one BB gun fight in the woods by the logging trail, when Richard took a hit above his left eyebrow—and, yes, *nearly* got his eye shot out . . .)—but we were *boys*, after all, and tended to give our babysitters (and our sisters, and our sisters' boyfriends) moments of aggravation.

The night in question was one of those nights. Margaret recalls it as "a sore point" in her "relationship to Dad," since she'd been left behind to manage our heady resistance to bedtime while he and Judy (home from college) had gone fishing.

I remember only that we were either told to stay *in* the house, but went out, or were told to stay *out*, and snuck back in. And that we were using for our ins and outs not only both the front (porch) door and back (kitchen) door of the gray-clapboard cottage, but the low, loose-screened windows of our bedroom as well. Whatever the initial circumstances, the game eventually became one of tease and rout, in and out, with Margaret the woeful target, the "it" of three rambunctious boys. In a kind of tag, or hide-and-seek, or Queen of the Cottage, Margaret was trying to capture us, and we taunted her by running past as she corralled one or two. But she couldn't get all three.

At some point in our game, as I was racing to get into the kitchen, launching up the back steps, I must have underestimated my velocity, for when I reached the storm door—which Margaret had perhaps locked—my right hand crashed through the glass.

I screamed, and yanked my hand back out through the shattered glass with an immediacy I've since witnessed only in video reversal. Poor judgment on my part, to be sure, as the exit likely caused more damage than the entrance. But *it hurt!* I remember a lot of glass shards and blood on the threshold and hemp door mat, on the kitchen linoleum, and in the sink. Blood that my sister couldn't at the time stomach very well (my sister who, in an odd twist of fate, would later in life become a nurse). Bleeding that couldn't be stopped. Since Margaret could not yet drive—nor could she leave my brothers unattended for any length of time—she phoned our Aunt Sue, a health and physical education teacher, certified in first aid, who rushed over from my grandmother's cottage down the lake and transported me to the Frankfort hospital, where

I received the first stitches I'd ever gotten. In what I later learned to call "quirky," four stitches went into my hand at geographically the same relative location as Frankfort is on Michigan's mitt. Four others went into my wrist, where the skin had pulled open enough to reveal a bulge of muscle, something, I recall, that simultaneously interested and nauseated me. (Something that, due to the stitches' premature removal and subsequent flesh-yawn, is a bulge of scar tissue to this day.)

It's not coincidence that poets define their lives in terms of physical objects, especially those that manifest familiar metaphorical qualities. The fragility of human existence is glass-like, able to shatter under certain pressure—yet, for all its thin transparency, it is solid nonetheless. And nonetheless beautiful, for both its surface and shatter, its drama and destruction. How often in films or TV dramas do we see the image of a body flying through a glass door or window—exploding walls of glass—the brilliant, unnatural sounds of it—replicated as a way to mark a climactic moment, a moment of significance, of passion, change, or finality. Of metaphor. How often is it at the same time displayed in slow-motion, visually-gorgeous cinematography, in contradistinction to the character's obvious trauma.

The widower in my poem, in considering his hand as the location of *home*, recounts *his* scars, which would be numerous, as anyone who's lived or worked on a farm would be able to attest. In doing so, he recounts as well the memories of hidden wounds, what are sometimes called "emotional scars." For the first time perhaps the widower realizes that distance will not remove those: that no matter how different the places are that he visits (cobblestone streets, barge canals, gothic cathedrals) or how different the people that he meets, his hands will always be a physiological record of his life—a legend, say, of luck and circumstance, of location and occupation.

In contemplating our hands, we may see our accomplishments, our triumphs, our accidents, our mistakes. Our losses. In such contemplation, may we not also note, beneath the topography of flesh, the poem of our being: moments of melancholy or nostalgia, stories of satisfaction and contentment, even happiness? Scars are, after all, what's left from *healing*.

There are a dozen or more smaller scars on the palm and wrist of my right hand from incidents of boy-play and restlessness during the time we lived in the cottage on Platte Lake. Scars from a relatively happy time of a relatively happy childhood. Over the years, I have added numerous other scars—in addition to countless mental and emotional souvenirs of broken bones and contusions, of heartache and loss—mementos of other times . . .

They are scars, I think now, as much of *place* as incident.

LOST & FOUND

We left Scarborough, Maine, about eight-thirty in the morning, heading northwest. Our intentions were to take Route 302 through New Hampshire and Vermont to Burlington, where we'd catch the ferry across Lake Champlain and then come down I-87 from there. But by the time we got to Wells River—after an hour's shopping spree at the L.L. Bean outlet in North Conway and a layover for a picnic lunch at the site of the Wiley House in Crawford Notch—we decided to shoot down I-91 instead and go across Vermont further south. We had taken a lot longer than we had planned to climb through the Presidential Range, and we had promised to be in upstate New York by the end of the week.

"From the White River Junction," said my wife Debbie, the atlas open on her lap, "we can take Route 4 through Rutland and pick up I-87 somewhere around Glens Falls."

"Okay by me," I said.

Which is how we came to stop at the Shell station outside Quechee at about three in the afternoon. As I pulled up to the pumps, two things caught my attention. At $1.12 a gallon, the price of gas was fairly competitive with what we'd paid in Connecticut and Maine, although it was considerably more expensive than what we were paying when we left Michigan in July. (Of course, what we didn't realize at the time—the summer of 1990—was that even as I pumped unleaded into our tank, Iraqi troops were moving across the desert toward Kuwait and by the end of the following week we'd be paying almost twenty cents a gallon more.)

The kids noticed the other thing: just beyond the station's tarmac, beyond the guardrail that barely delineated where the properties divided, in a potholed and dusty parking lot, stood two racks and a table piled with books—used books—mostly paperbacks. The older kids begged to go and see if there were any they could buy. They had already read—twice—every Hardy Boys and Babysitter Club book in the car, and they were willing, they said, to spend their own money (which we had given them the week before—for souvenirs).

"You'd better be ready when I am," I said, after Debbie reminded me that we had no reservations for the night and that the afternoon was pressing on.

We shepherded the two younger children to the restrooms and I bought soda pop for everyone. Then I moved the van nearer the barn-like structure into which Rachel and Matthew had disappeared. A minor-league book collector myself—what literature professor isn't?—I was interested in seeing what might be inside, although I couldn't believe there'd be anything of value, given the looks of the outside. The building appeared to have been a storage shed that had outworn its usefulness. The outside walls were paint-flaked and sun-bleached, with obviously temporary or last-minute repairs—a new board nailed here or there. I think the roof was stained tarpaper or rusty metal. Hand-painted on the door were letters that simply spelled *BOOKS*, and stapled on the walls around the door were an assortment of multi-colored fliers and posters advertising everything from missing children to concerts in the park; I doubted if the posters were even current. If the place had a name, I imagine it was something quaint and unpretentious, like "Bill's Books" or "The Book Shack." But I don't recall seeing any sign.

The paperback selections in the parking lot were just what I expected, the kinds of books we often found at library or AAUW book sales—Anne Tyler, Sidney Sheldon, Danielle Steele, Stephen King. If those were any indication of what juvenile selections might be inside, I was fairly certain that the kids would find themselves some good deals.

The inside of the shack mimicked the outside in its structure—it was functional, not aesthetic. The aisles were narrow and dim, even as the sun glared through the poorly hung door. The shelves were constructed of unfinished boards, nailed at various heights, and old greeting card racks, the type you'd find at flea markets. There was barely enough room for two people to pass between the stacks, which reached to the ceiling. The place was nearly what I had expected.

What I hadn't expected was the number and variety of books. There were the requisite used comic books, of course, and dime store paperbacks like the ones in the parking lot. But there were also first editions, collector's editions, hardbound, leather-bound, reference, how-to, cookbooks, gardening books, juvenile, biography, history, art, auto repair, catalogs—more books than I believed could even fit in such a place.

There were books like the well-thumbed mysteries I used to find at my grandmother's cottage. (The ones you'd open and a photograph would fall to the braided rug—a yellowed photograph of a boy holding a stringer of perch, bass, or pickerel arranged according to size, the boy's front teeth missing in a fish-like grin. Something about the face would be familiar, but it would take some study before I'd recognize my uncle's deep-set eyes and gleaming ears.) And yet not two shelves away there were books like Crowell's Red Line Poets Series, with their "Gilt edges, red line borders, illustrated, and bound in beautiful designs"—like *Familiar Quotations, Poetry of Flowers, Lady of the Lake, Surf and Wave*—several of the volumes hand-inscribed on the frontispiece in fountain pen ink ("Compliments of R.J.S. Dec. 1886"). The shack was a bibliophile's heaven.

My interest was stirred. Out of curiosity I asked the tall, thin, blond, bespectacled young man behind the counter (where a small dirty portable radio played classical music) if he had any contemporary poetry. I was expecting to find, as I often do, a couple high school anthologies and maybe some Robert Frost. (After all, we were in *his* New England.) What the clerk directed me to was a corner nook the whole wall of which—floor to ceiling—was crowded with poetry. Not only were Robert Frost and Edwin Arlington Robinson represented, but there were books by Edna St. Vincent Millay, William Carlos Williams, Ezra Pound, Charles Olson, Elizabeth Bishop, Marianne Moore, and Wallace Stevens, as well as Galway Kinnell, Donald Hall, Gerald Stern, Howard Moss, John Ashbery, Linda Pastan, Robert Bly, Sharon Olds, and scores of others. Some books were dog-eared and annotated, as though they had been used in college courses; some were hardbound and covered in clean new jackets, as though they had never been read.

There were anthologies too—from Brooks and Warrens' classic *Understanding Poetry* to Donald Allen's *New American Poetry*. In addition, to my surprise, I found a healthy selection of recent small magazines and journals, both familiar (*New England Review, Ploughshares, New York Quarterly*) and unfamiliar. There were even single issues of pamphlets that I had never heard of—some nothing more than stenciled copies folded and stapled. The nook was a Lost and Found for poetry.

Once I overcame my initial surprise, I took a few minutes to flip through whatever looked interesting, reading poems at random. Then, when I saw on one of the highest shelves an unprinted cream-yellow spine that looked strangely similar to something I had on my bookshelf at home, I enlisted the help of a folding step-stool—a number of which were leaning at strategic locations all around the store—and reached down a copy of *handsel*. At that point, I had one of those chilling moments of epiphany, or déjà vu, like when we feel we have returned to a place we'd never been before. My face flushed with astonishment and coincidence.

For a few years in the early 1970s *handsel* had been edited by Gray Zeitz and Coy Holstein and published out of Lexington, Kentucky. It was primarily regional in its distribution; I had discovered it when my faculty advisor at Centre College, in Danville, directed me to a call for submissions. *handsel* was the first *real* literary magazine I submitted poems to (that is, not affiliated with the school I was attending). The first to publish me.

I don't imagine that more than a couple hundred copies of any issue of *handsel* were printed. And while the quality of the magazine may have improved with every issue, the earliest copy I have is inexpensively duplicated on legal-size paper, folded and stapled, with a card-stock cover. It was nothing very fancy. Yet I can still recall my thrill at receiving my contributor's copy, in spite of it being obviously low-budget, temporary and frail. I was *published*, and I felt good about it. What did I care if, over the next ten years, when I had the rare occasion to acknowledge *handsel* in my short bio, very few people had ever heard of it? After graduating from Centre and moving back to Michigan, I lost track of the magazine. Years later, I assumed *handsel* had gone by the wayside, as did many of the small literary ventures that first published me.

Now we were together again, twenty-odd years later, in the most obscure and remote bookstore that I've ever stumbled upon, and here I was feeling the same thrill I felt seeing my first poem in print. I was feeling strong and proud; I was feeling affirmed, literary. I was feeling accomplished. Finding my poetic self again—if only by the circumstantial changing of directions mid-day—says something about the lasting quality of poetry, even as we acknowledge the transitory and ephemeral nature of publishing.

That's not to say that early poems don't embarrass me, that I haven't also developed an aesthetic disfavor for those early and often faulty poems after so many years. In their rediscovery, I am painfully reminded of my adolescent blather, of my insensate poetic immaturity, and I'm often tempted to buy the magazines in which they appear and destroy them, in the way I have destroyed (discarded) the original typed copies/drafts of the poems. After all, they had been lost to me for years, so what possible value could they have for someone else? These less-than-perfect poems . . .

At the same time, I am astonished by my rediscovery of the energy that I had confidently loosed upon the world twenty years before, and how the poems themselves seem to have lived well enough alone after I freed them. The energy of creativity must be a sustaining power.

When I showed *handsel* to Debbie and the children, they were excited, and yet, the intrinsic, ambiguous value of rediscovery that I was feeling seemed secondary to their interest in the present. The person whose name was in print stood before them, but to them the poems were simply "Daddy's." That was all the connection they cared about.

"Why don't you buy it?" Debbie said. "It may be valuable, like an antique."

I considered it.

In the end, I decided to leave that issue of *handsel* in Quechee, Vermont, for someone else to find—maybe a stranger, who may rejoice in the thrill of first discovery—or someone like Roff McEwen or T. Reynolds or Barbara Jean Shallal or Thomas Stegal or E. Sure or "Gus's friend from Louisiana" or any of the other poets listed with me on the contributor's page. Maybe one of them will accidentally and unexpectedly find *handsel* in a remote bookstore in some city or small town where they've never been, and they'll be taken back to a time when poetry was important to them and pleasurable. Maybe they're lawyers now or dentists or insurance salesmen or realtors and in discovering a poem from another time in their life they'll rediscover a part of themselves that they had lost in the hubbub of their mad routines. Maybe they'll rediscover how pleasure can be regenerated by *intent* rather than simply *coincidence* and they'll begin to write again.

I squeezed *handsel* back on the second shelf from the ceiling and left it there, like a practical joke waiting for some unsuspecting stooge.

As it turned out, we didn't buy anything at all at the book shack. We drove on to Woodstock and then north to Barnard, where we tented in a campground overlooking Silver Lake. Later that night, sitting in the moonlight near the fire, I found myself giving a lot of thought to our stop at the book shack, to the accident of rediscovery, the coincidence of poetry.

Some writers have argued that we need to be more careful with what we bring into this world—as Mary Wollstonecraft Shelley so well understood. Unlike fads or fashion, unlike styles, unlike even the tenuous nature of our human flesh, art never dies. Even bad art. To look back at a creation that makes me embarrassed or ashamed and to think that such poetry will outlive me is, at best, depressing. At worst, it's frightening and monstrous. Especially today, with the exponential proliferation of writing programs and online (daily) publications—literature as consumer goods—maybe we need to reconsider our production—the bland and self-indulgent nature of American poetry today. Will our literary offspring be embarrassed or ashamed two hundred years from now?

Others argue that maybe we need to be more care*free* with what we bring into the world, knowing that it will survive well enough on its own, that no matter how ugly or delinquent our offspring might be, we'll still find a thrill in our awareness that we can create offspring at all—in our rediscovery of our creative power. No matter how lost or neglected individual poems may be, the intrinsic energy of Poetry will sustain them.

Co-incidence: maybe we can have it both ways.

We reached Morningsun Farm in the Finger Lakes region of New York on Saturday, and, to our unbound pleasure, our friends greeted us like rediscovered poems.

HOW I WRITE POETRY

First, I make sure I have enough gas. If I don't, I take the one-gallon can to Wesco and put a dollar's worth of unleaded into it. While I'm there, I might buy a candy bar and flip through the most recent magazines.

Next, I check the oil. If the dipstick is dry, I add enough 10W30 to bring the level up to the cross-hatched safety zone. If I don't have enough oil, I'll run over to Auto Works and buy a quart. I may also stop at Great Lakes Books to see what may be on sale.

After I get home, I empty the plastic kids' pool of rainwater and drowned yellow jackets and move it off the grass. I make sure the lawn chairs, Frisbees, soccer balls, bikes, and sandbox toys are either on the deck or in the driveway. I coil the garden hose and cover the sandbox with a blue tarp.

About then, Andrew will want a push on the swing, so I'll invest a few minutes in teaching him to pump with his legs, calculating the day when he'll swing by himself—the return on my investment. Sarah will come outside to hang upside down on the bars and will ask me if she can see if Robin can play, but I'll remember that Rachel needs to be taken to piano lessons, so I'll load into the Caravan any kids that can't be left at home alone and I'll deliver

Rachel to Mrs. Wismer's. Fortunately, I won't need to stay; Debbie will pick up Rachel on her way home from work.

Back at the house, Matthew needs help subtracting decimals. Sarah is off on her bike. Andrew wants someone to "play Legos" with him.

"But when am I going to cut the grass?" I ask, rhetorically.

Matthew volunteers—to play Legos with Andrew.

So I return to the yard.

My secondhand Sears power mower starts easily, if I remember to pump the choke fifteen or twenty times. Then, for the next couple hours—give or take a half-dozen stops to scribble a phone message or throw a pot-roast in the oven, or mix Kool-Aid—I will push and pull, grunt and groan, cough and sneeze, curse, and, essentially, ignore everything but the mowing. For the better part of those two hours, the roar from the engine will muffle most distractions, and what the kids call my 'mad-eyebrow' facial expression will dissuade all but the most serious of interruptions. Should the Muse want to reach me, that is to say, my phone lines are open. I call it *writing*.

I'll do anything in order to avoid facing the stare of cotton bond. I'll clean the oven or fold socks. I'll return books to the library or make a special trip across town for guinea pig food. I've even been known to remodel a house completely—inside and out, from shingle to subfloor—in order to avoid writing. I'll take the kids to the pool or beach ("because they *deserve* it" is my excuse). Or to the ice cream store. Or to Paris Park to feed the trout. I'll cut coupons out of newspapers. I'll go to the neighbors and borrow their newspapers in order to cut out the coupons. *Anything*. To avoid writing a poem.

In contrast to the advice of many "professional" writers—like journalists and novelists—who argue that a person should "write regularly, every day," I tell a person who wants to write poetry to stop writing altogether. Cold turkey.

Like giving up cigarettes.

If you're lucky, you'll never write another poem. Your life will be free of addiction—that is to say, you'll have no grass to cut, like a perennial day at the beach. But if you're unlucky, if you're meant to be a poet, you'll never make it. Every book at the consignment store will raise your arm hairs in gooseflesh; every blank notepad will sing; every *beep* from a keyboard or *click* of a typewriter will cause you to break into a cold sweat. Writing will weigh upon your heart like sickness. Eventually you'll have to sneak off to cop a poem or sell your sleep to shoot up a story. Of course you'll curse the cursed need to write—at which your loved ones will sigh—and then you'll give in to it completely and write and rewrite as though you'd never write enough.

That's what happens when we avoid writing, if we're true writers. There's no release. Our avoidance itself becomes a squeak in the ear-buzz of our mowing—a word, a phrase or two, a rhyme, a couple lines—and before we know it we're chanting among the scattered heads of dandelions, throwing our grassy excuses to the wind.

No amount of "wanting" will make a writer write. Instead, like pregnancy, the more we want it, the more difficult it seems to become.

So I say, "Avoid it." If the writing comes, it will come when it's ready—magically, mysteriously, with sublime awe. If we ignore it, if we don't allow it to make its demands upon us, if we keep ourselves busy, the poems will come—when they're ready, when we least expect them: a word or phrase will break water into being, cry out, and gulp its first breath of air.

Resign yourself to it, I say. Your busy, demanding life will never be the same.

SANDBURG AND ME

Carl Sandburg appeared to me—miraculously—in 1971, as I made my way across the campus of Centre College. I was a junior that year and tightly scheduled, having declared majors in both English and studio art, and so, as I trekked from the natatorium, where I had just finished teaching a lifesaving course for the local Red Cross, to the Cowan Dining Hall for a quick snack, I swung through the post office to verify that my mailbox was empty, as it usually was. Except for holiday or birthday cards, or the rare brief note and "extra" five-dollar bill from my father, Box 1015 was typically nothing more than a narrow, square telescope into the inner workings of the mailroom. But on that particular morning, my view was hindered by what appeared to be a fat letter, wedged in the box at an awkward angle. How exciting! So much so that I fumbled the combination several times before I was able to remove a plain, stationary-sized envelope of uncommon girth addressed simply to "1015." At first, I assumed my mailbox had been confused with someone else's—which happened occasionally and could be blamed on the work-study nature of college postal employees—yet when I peeled up the flap of the envelope and pulled out the enclosure, I was sure it was meant for me.

Unfolded, the heavy paper measures approximately ten-and-a half by fourteen inches and—by the various creases and glued overlap and general design—appears to have led a former life as a small brown grocery sack, the color of the Kentucky River at flood stage. On the right side of the front, Carl Sandburg's head is reproduced in a "wash" of India ink. His face is in semi-profile; he appears to be looking over my left shoulder, in a contemplative, poetic way, as if he is considering what words of advice he might provide—what words of poetry—words that would be selected for me, and me alone, with considerable care and intent (or so I thought at the time).

To the left of Sandburg's profile—a quarter turn of his head and he would be facing them—are three selections from his poetry, typed methodically onto the thick brown paper. The uppermost selection begins: "There must be a place / a room and a sanctuary / set apart for silence . . ."

I continued to the dining hall, reading the selections as I walked—concerned about getting something to drink, at least, before Dr. Sweeney's medieval lit class—when my attention was drawn back to the look on Sandburg's face. The eyes are clearly those of a poet: they are wise and calm, and provide a look of affirmation, of possibility. But most of all, they are patient eyes. The artist's talent, I thought, was remarkable (but for the slightly elephantine left ear, which seems to have posed some problems—though surely to be excused, given the challenges of drawing in indelible ink!).

At Walnut Street, I stopped—as if to wait for traffic to clear (though there wasn't any)—and turned the paper over. On the back side was a note, written in pencil, in cursive, the margins unjustified and irregularly lineated.

Over the years, the writing has faded—the text is now faint—yet the message remains as pronounced as the day I pulled the fat envelope from my mailbox:

There's something
about the heavy texture of
brown paper that suits my nature
There's something about the rough
& unfinished quality that suggest warmth
and humility
There's something about C. Sandburg's poems
that captures my thoughts & expresses me
when I cannot express myself

Is it wrong to give a poet a poem?
I like Carl Sandburg's <u>next</u> to yours.
I'd really like to say congratulations
on having one of your works accepted for publication.

I send you this because I really have
nothing more to give right now

and because you will understand it, while others won't.
and because some of it suits your nature, too
(at least, as I understand it—although it's possible
I don't)

No signature appears anywhere on the brown paper, not on either side, not on the envelope. There are no initials. No hints at who the artist, or the author of the note, might be.

I will admit here that Carl Sandburg has never been my favorite poet, despite spending much of the rest of that afternoon reading and rereading the Sandburg selections in my *Norton Anthology* and then hours in the Doherty Library exploring what works of Sandburg's were available there. Yet the thought that Sandburg's poems had expressed *something* that could not be expressed in any other way—to such an extent that someone painstakingly typed out selections and sent them to me [if you've ever tried to insert a grocery bag into a manual typewriter, you'll understand what I mean by "painstakingly"]—motivated me to return to Sandburg's poems again and again, trying to figure it out. Which led me, naturally, to other books of poetry on those library shelves, other poets I was not familiar with . . .

Is it wrong to give a poet a poem?

It was, unquestionably, the first time that anyone—especially someone I didn't know, a stranger to me—confirmed my membership in the brotherhood of poets [an arguably acceptable collective noun at that time, though the "sisterhood" was burgeoning and would come into prominence in the next three decades]. I was both cheered and humbled by the confirmation. While at the time I *wanted* to see myself as a poet, and for other people to see me as one, I was also insecure enough (or arrogant enough) to play down the role. I was merely a student after all, a beginner. And yet there is something in the look of Carl Sandburg's eyes that generated in me—germinated—a certain confidence in that rhetorical question. A confidence that soon encouraged me to "pay it forward," to pass that confirmation along—often anonymously—with not only my own poems but with the poems of many poets I've discovered since and have come to love—passed to my friends, to colleagues, to members of my family, to my students . . . occasionally, even, accompanied by a work of original art (although by my senior year at Centre it was clear I was not meant to be a visual artist).

No, it is not wrong to give *anyone* a poem, as the Academy of American Poets advocates during National Poetry Month. With poetry, as much as with anything, *to give* is *to receive*. Particularly when the gift is anonymous.

Carl has seen better days, of course. He accompanied me during my graduate work at Central Michigan and Bowling Green State University; he was pinned to the corkboard above my office desk for eight years at Keuka College, and then, for twenty-six years, followed me from one office to another (taped and retaped, or push pinned) at Ferris State University, from which we retired together in 2013. His brown paper has aged, has ripped in places, has been creased and recreased many times. There are multiple holes in the two corners that are still intact; the other two corners have chunks missing, ripped from over-adhesion or careless removal. The back of the paper is reinforced at places with white tape; the penciled message (reproduced above) is nearly illegible. The heft that grocery bag paper tends to have when it's new has been worn to the thinness of an aerogram. And there is a significant tear in the middle of the front, from Carl's forehead to the words "There must be substance here": the word *here* itself separated in two. (I'm smiling at the irony . . .)

If I ever had an inkling, a suspicion, of who introduced Carl Sandburg to me, I no longer recall. I suppose that over the years there must have been times when I looked up at Carl on the wall above my desk and wished that I knew—wished, in fact, that the person who gave me Carl had fessed up to it and that it was a person whom I had secretly admired from a distance, and who—like

Carl—would suddenly appear at my office door, or somewhere, and . . . well, you've seen enough movies to get the idea. Surely there were also moments of poetic doubt, of vulnerability, of failure. But they were brief and passing. More often, when I looked into Sandburg's eyes—or read his poetry—I gathered from him a knowledge of patience and strength, of endurance.

Today, I don't care to know who exactly put Carl Sandburg in my mailbox. The gift in fact may as well have been given by any number of people I met at Centre—or since then—friend, colleague, acquaintance, stranger, male or female—a person who for some reason wanted to assume anonymity but by giving me an ink-washed portrait of Carl Sandburg became, instead, an intimate, a lover. Someone who knew the poetry that lives in all of us.

MONKEY BUSINESS

I step onto the deck I built off the back of my house years ago and for the first time notice that there are no monkeys in my trees. There are no colobus monkeys, no capuchin-like monkeys—no spider, woolly, or howler monkeys—and no macaques. I return inside, retrieve my binoculars from the dining room table, and then step out again to confirm it. There are no signs of monkeys in any of the maple, willow, evergreen, flowering crab, or thornapple trees on the quarter-acre behind the house. Nor are there monkeys in my oversized oak, which not only defines the far edge of my rowdy yard but stands well above the rest. I'm astonished. I've owned this property in Big Rapids Township for the better part of eighteen years, and it is only now that I've taken to notice the absence of monkeys.

The reason, it suddenly occurred to me, must be a literary one.

What had launched me onto the deck in the first place, what had caused me to search for small primates among the branches of my familiar trees, was Ezra Pound's poem "The River Merchant's Wife: A Letter," which I'd been reading. I've taught Pound's poem dozens of times in my years of teaching—maybe more than dozens, if I count the semesters I offered multiple sections of American lit and the years I used the poem in more than one semester, not to mention the times I've alluded to "The River Merchant's Wife" in community or public school poetry workshops. Yet, in all that time, I'd never before considered the poem outside of the context in which I was teaching it. I'd never considered what I wasn't hearing.

In Pound's poem, "The monkeys make sorrowful noise overhead." The line stands out for its poignancy, capturing with uncanny simplicity the sadness and longing that the river merchant's wife feels. Her young husband, whom she desires to mingle her dust with "forever and forever and forever," has been gone for five long months, and she grieves his absence.

It is an absence I'm familiar with. Five months ago, I packed off to college the last of my four children (custody of which I "won" in the divorce), and so now live solitary among ghost-laughs. I am convinced, through the transliteration of his poem, that Pound was familiar with such absence as well, regardless of the fact that, like myself, he may never have heard monkeys in the wild and so really could not have known whether they were sorrowful or not. To be sure, the majority of Pound's readers would have very little experience with the emotive (let alone linguistic) meaning of the shrieks and grunts and hubbub of our specious cousins, given that our exposure is likely limited to the cacophony of monkey islands at various zoos or safari parks or from the dubbed or canned monkeyspeak of Disney TV shows or Tarzan movies.

And so, one might ask, how can I possibly know, *as I do*, what sounds the river merchant's wife hears overhead? I know because at times the trees in my yard make such noises. They are times, like today, when, in order to escape from the wrench of loneliness, brought on by my solitary reading, I am jolted from my blue chair, and I seek some affirmation of *being*, if not belonging. I take to the deck and listen. In the slightest wind my trees cry and moan, creak and whistle. It is the sound of the trees' empty branches.

Like a dove's mournful coo, you might say. But no, it is not the sound of mourning, despite the dove's namesake, though some birds do make a noise like grieving widows. (A trope, I'd argue, all too familiar in American backyards and literary texts.) Granted, there is demonstrative sorrow in bird language: a sorrow of flocks and bevies, of gaggles and murders, a sorrow of dole and flight and piteousness, a sorrow of charm and fleet . . . And yet, in its very ubiquity, such sorrow is rife with self-pity and civic harmony. It is a public sorrow. It is not what I hear. What I hear is more exotic and unfamiliar, a noise that manifests itself so appropriately in Pound's image that I am moved by it. In part because I do not know what it is, its absence charges my imagination.

"And *yet*," you interrupt, "monkeys are among the most social of mammals. Wouldn't dismissing birdsong for its antiphonal symphony, its aggregate suffering, require us to dismiss as well the communal dirge of a monkey troop?" Not necessarily, I will answer. For it is not the monkeys *themselves* who are sorrowful; it is the river merchant's wife. To her, the noise—a noise familiar to her—has suddenly become sorrowful.

In literary terms, we call such projection *pathetic fallacy*, and I suppose that in Pound's poem the image of monkeys making sorrowful noise overhead could be excused as such. The monkeys are likely not making any different noises than they were before; what has changed is the river merchant's wife's perception. In her lover's absence, *everything* bespeaks of sorrow—the different mosses, the paired butterflies . . . even time. Consequently, accepting that the noises the monkeys make is suddenly recognized as sorrowful (as if they hadn't always been), assumes on the reader's part an acceptance of the speaker's familiarity with monkey noise. What was once familiar is suddenly redefined in a way that makes it *unfamiliar*. Makes it new. Even startling. We find meaning where there hadn't been meaning before. We are moved by what we realize is *not* there; what we realize, of course, is *poetry*.

It was then, when I considered how quiet the house was without my children, that I took to my deck and looked for the first time into my trees. There are no monkeys, and their absence makes a sorrowful noise.

V.

I am chilled with reminiscence.

MODEL CLASSROOM

Twenty-seven fourth graders hunch in the five rows of desks the volunteer docent at the Michigan History Museum called "antique." We chaperones idle in the back, pretending not to be there—seven women of childbearing age (five guardians, a disability paraprofessional, the students' teacher) and me. I stand out as one of only two adult males in attendance, the other being our elderly docent, who introduces himself as "Mr. John." By my estimation, I am also the second oldest person in the room (after Mr. John).

"Comfortable?" Mr. John asks. It's a rhetorical question, to signal that he's ready to begin, and the fourth graders, seasoned to field trips, nod politely. "Good," he continues, launching into a well-rehearsed explanation of how the desks the students are sitting in were typical of rural Michigan schools "back in the day"—a time Mr. John doesn't specify exactly, though I could date as the early twentieth century, given how familiar the desks appear—an unquestionable precursor to the desk design of the 1950s, my own elementary years.

All at once I feel as if two of the larger boys had just hefted open an institutional-sized multipaned window. I am chilled with reminiscence. In place of the desks before me I can see tubular steel frames welded into coat-hanger shaped legs, the desk-end legs slightly wider than those supporting the seat, which consists of a single plywood base and two meagerly curved slats as a back rest. ("Designed to teach proper posture . . .") The desk "tops"—one-inch-thick hardwood boards—are hinged about four inches from the front end of the desk, which is affixed to a cloudy-gray rectangular metal bin, its sides angled in a way to allow for a sloped writing surface. The center of the four-inch-wide level and stationary piece of wood at the front of the desk has been routed out about a quarter-inch deep and twelve inches long, to provide a place where pencils won't tumble onto the floor. That hole at the top right-hand side—Mr. John explains, since none of the students seems to know—is an inkwell, where a small metal basket was suspended to hold bottles of black or deep blue ink.

Mr. John seems to be speaking from experience when he talks about education in those days, especially how much emphasis was placed on penmanship ("cursive," he calls it), which you were taught to do with your right hand. If you were left-handed, as he was, the teachers would sometimes tie your left hand behind your back, so you'd learn how to do it right.

He then offers to answer any questions.

Jenny—whose mother on the bus ride to the museum had shared stories about watching the TV version of *Little House on the Prairie* when she was Jenny's age—wonders if teachers really whacked your hands with a stick if you didn't behave.

Mr. John replies that methods of discipline were certainly different back then.

Henry, the one student you could always count on to participate—bright for his age and comfortable around adults—asks whether it was called *writing* because you were taught to do it with your *right* hand.

The women chuckle knowingly. Even the mother who had been texting from the moment we'd entered the classroom (and who looks like she could be Henry's mother) smiles a perceptive, condescending smile. But Mr. John takes the question in stride. "A different kind of *right*," he says, teacherly, spelling each word.

Henry looks embarrassed, and I feel bad for him.

I recall how uncomfortable those desks were, how impossible it was to write neatly on the slanted tops, especially given all the carvings and etchings in the wood—the initials, the cuss words, the scratched-out hearts, the dates from years before—and how easily the screws that held the hinges could be removed so when the next student lifted the writing surface to pull out her grammar book, the whole top of the desk would crash shockingly to the floor.

I failed penmanship in fourth grade, in spite of the additional practice I was assigned during lunch break, when I was more likely to spend my time trapping drowsy houseflies so as to divest them of their wings (which I had a certain talent for). Even as a right-hander, I could never get penmanship right. My small *g*'s looked like *q*'s, my capital *S*'s like *G*'s. My loops were lopsided, my *I*'s like italics on a drunken binge. There was no consistency, no recognizable pattern. I had no patience for getting it right.

In the end, I mixed cursive with printing, designed my own font (so to speak), a font that is so irregular and moody to this day that I occasionally have to decipher it even for people who know me, and who forgive me for my public school transgressions, and who claim to admire how—beyond school—I learned to write so well.

CULTURE *CHOC*

According to a fact sheet supplied by the United States Information Agency, the Fulbright Program—the U.S. Government's international educational exchange program—is designed "to increase mutual understanding between the people of the United States and the people of other countries." In my experience as a Fulbright Lecturer at the University of Liège, Belgium, in 1992-93, that's easier said than done. In my case, "mutual understanding" would translate better as "mutual confusion." But then, translation itself may be part of the problem.

If it's true that people learn by making mistakes, I have become an expert on Belgian customs and social traditions. Take kissing as one example. In Belgium, casual acquaintances greet each other with a kiss on the right cheek. (Actually, in many instances it's a brush of cheek while making a kissing sound.) Children often greet adults with such a kiss even if they're not familiars.

I, for one, was not prepared for this type of greeting. During the weeks before our move to Liège, I had practiced the Cordial Handshake—a greeting itself that does not come naturally to the offspring of physically conservative parents (socially speaking) but which I had been assured would be the appropriate European greeting. So the first time the young son of one of my colleagues at the university greeted me, that is, made a move to kiss my cheek, I was caught off guard. I thought he was going to bite my ear. I didn't know what to do. So I grabbed his hand and shook it cordially, which no doubt confused him.

Our children encountered much the same, in spades. The first few days attending school at *Institut Sainte-Marie* they were kissed repeatedly as the other children jockeyed for friendships with the only American students they'd ever met. And without a defensive handshake or a polite way to communicate "Non, merci," they were resigned to wiping off their cheeks when no one was looking. Unfortunately, they were the perfect size for youthful kissing (unlike me, who could avoid a snotty nose by just not bending down). So it was a sloppy first few days, until they learned to compromise. In a short time they became selective kissers (of friends) and feigned cultural ignorance to all others. Much like the Belgians themselves.

Of course, it's just when you think you have a custom figured out that it changes. With more intmate friends it's THREE kisses—right, left, right—especially if the kisser is very fond of the kissee or wants to make a good impression. Or if you're from Luxembourg. Luxembourgers kiss three times for a *normal* greeting. We discovered that the weekend the Benelux Fulbright Commission hosted a tour to the small neighboring country where nearly half of the people we met had head colds. That's when "mutual understanding" became translated as "Does anyone have Kleenex?"

While I can attribute some of my family's confusion to simple cultural exchange or *shock* (spelled *choc*, in French)—that is, a certain wallowing in unfamiliar social customs—I think much of my problem may not have been in the shock itself but in how some of us

Michiganders underestimate our adaptability. ("What does not change," writes the poet Charles Olson, "is the willingness to change.") One thing I thought we'd have trouble with—the food—wasn't a serious problem. I had expected from State-side experience that it would be unlikely we could satisfy the predilections of four finicky children when it came to foreign foods. I assumed that in a country promoting "gastronomic delights"—pickled eels, fish stew, wild rabbit, who-knows-what's-in-it pates and sausages—we'd have trouble getting the kids to eat. But I was wrong. The kids adjusted quite well. With food, "mutual understanding" came to mean, "Try a bite but don't ask what it is." What tasted good, we ate; what didn't, we cut up and left in small piles on our plates, as though we ate some of it. (Sarah, the pickiest, became adept at this deception and continued to practice it—with increasing regularity—upon our return to the States.)

Not to mention that chocolate is a staple of the Belgian diet.

We soon learned that there's no way even picky eaters would starve in Belgium. Belgians are known for their *frites* (French fries) which they serve as a side dish with nearly every meal or with a dollop of mayonnaise as a meal-in-itself. There were two *friteries* on our short block alone. The most popular day of the week at *Sainte-Marie* was Tuesday, when your child could order frites for hot lunch. And pasta and pizza are globally available. And Coke—although in Belgium it generally comes with a slice of lemon and no ice.

It was easier adapting to the food, in fact, than the language.[1] The kids learned French readily, as it was spoken all

---

[1] Again, on my part, assuming a homo-linguistic American standard may have been partly to blame.

day at school, their communication much supplemented with Belgian gestures, which they picked up from classmates. (Talk about a learning curve! Some of the gestures were clearly *not* to be used in formal contexts, like our meeting with the American Ambassador to Belgium.) Andrew, our youngest, who attended first level (or grade) at *Sainte-Marie*, the stage Belgian children learned to read and write in their "native" language, became particularly adept in French.[2]

But me, having taken French classes as an undergraduate years before (and for one semester as a student in Paris), and then barely passing the second-language "proficiency" exam as a Ph.D. candidate, I can read French competently enough, but I'm disinclined to speak it, as my pronunciation belies not only my Midwest American English but my Scots ancestry as well (if you can imagine). So I translate everything as I go. It's a frustrating and arduous process. And it's in that process of visual translation that I get into trouble with pronunciation. While few Belgians in Liège spoke English fluently[3]—unlike Brussels or other cities in Dutch-speaking Flanders—many had at least some English in school. So whenever I attempted to communicate orally—assassinating French freely—the shopkeepers or bank clerks often responded in English

---

[2] Liege is located in Walloon, the Francophone region of Belgium. Andrew learned to read and write French before he learned to read and write English, which he eventually would in second grade back in Big Rapids, under the patient tutelage of Mrs. Anderson, who had some experience in ESL.

[3] Obviously much has changed in the past thirty years, with digital TV and Internet, English being one of the standard languages of global media.

or else called for someone more bi-lingual. So much for the exchange being "mutual."

At the same time, I can't blame them. By translating everything literally, my dialect had resorted to a kind of pigeon-French—English sentences with French words. Which is especially bad when I'm talking on the phone (something I don't particularly care to do even in my native English). One day, for instance, I had telephoned the parents of my daughter's friend Severine to see if Severine could come over on Saturday. By the time I was done, the young, French-speaking members of the family who had overheard my conversation were laughing uncontrollably. Apparently, I had told Severine's father that I'd have to walk her home because I didn't have a vulture.

My mistake. I meant the French word for car, *la voiture*.

At least what's lacking in cultural exchange is made up in entertainment, though I'm not sure Severine's family got as big a chuckle out of my *faux pas* as my children.

If the Fulbright Program is designed to promote "mutual understanding," I think they may have sent the wrong person. I seem to promote more mutual confusion than anything else. I can only hope that some *cultural* understanding—or education—will be the end result, if I can make enough mistakes.

MAJDANEK

I visited Majdanek twice during the academic year 1996-97, when I lived in Lublin, Poland, where I was teaching as a Fulbright Professor at Marie Curie-Skłodowska University. The first time was during Christmas break, when Andrzej Chodkiewicz, husband of my colleague Halina, thought it would be educational for my two older children, Matthew and Rachel, who were visiting for the holiday, to experience one vestige of Poland's sad history. Marta Chodkiewicz, small enough to squeeze in the four-passenger car with us, went along as translator. The Chodkiewicz family had spent a year in the States under the Fulbright Program (as Halina completed research on English pedagogy), and so 13-year-old Marta, having attended public school in Illinois, spoke English quite well. Andrzej claimed to have lost his facility to speak English, often deferring to Halina's expertise (though he comprehended quite a lot), and what little Polish I had, despite weekly lessons, returned little more than blank stares from my students and shopkeepers.

It was a short drive to the "museum." Unlike the more infamous Auschwitz, which the Nazis established at the deserted pre-war Polish barracks in Oświçim because of the location's remoteness and isolation, the "camp" at Majdanek was laid out in cabbage fields within walking distance of Lublin's central railway station, along the far end of two city bus routes. As a result, Majdanek is an immediate and constant reminder to Lublin residents of World War II, the Holocaust, and foreign occupation (among other things). Given such proximity, I expected to find a tastefully reconstructed open air museum, along the lines of the "State Museum in Oświçim" (Auschwitz-Birkenau) or even Sachsenhausen, the museum at the former camp near Berlin, both of which I'd previously toured. But there is no "tour" at Majdanek.[4]

The "museum" consists of a dozen or so former barracks, two concrete monuments, several kilometers of barbed wire fencing (in double rows), a few guard towers, and one remaining crematorium. There is also a small information center, but it was closed on that particular day, the Sunday after Christmas.

One monument stands at the entrance. It consists of a pit or cavern carved out of a huge concrete base, through which a visitor may descend (somewhat arduously). At the far end of the pit, just beyond steep ascending stairs, a bus-sized monolith looms, suspended horizontally on two stocky pillars. The monolith is an ungainly, weather-worn bas-relief, suggesting perhaps distorted bodies and faces in various forms of agony. Great slabs of rock appear to be whacked out of the sculpture and distributed as obstacles in the carved-out valley. On the day we visited, this "entrance" was unsettling, ominous and grotesque against the drab winter sky, not only for its size and improbability but for its damp, uretic smell.

[4] This may have changed in the twenty years since this essay was first drafted.

From there, a hike of a kilometer or so along the double rows of barbed-wire fencing and guard towers brought us to the other monument, a flying saucer-shaped dome that hovered just above a small rise at the far corner of what's been left of the camp. On our way, we passed a dozen black barn-like buildings in neat rows, indistinguishable but for their numbers. But we met no other people; there were no signs of life at all. Except for us, the "museum" was deserted, making it somewhat difficult to imagine the many thousands of prisoners who had been crammed into those buildings, four to six bodies in bunk space no larger than a double door, or lined up eight deep to use one of the horse-trough urinals. At the same time, it was not so difficult to imagine how miserable they had been, for the cold dreariness of the place cut through us, despite our Columbia jackets and Lands' End sweaters.

We hurried behind Marta, who seemed anxious to get us through the place as fast as she could. She fielded our questions gamely, but neither she nor her father appeared very knowledgeable about the camp, despite its proximity to Lublin. Not until Andzrej tracked down one of the "guards," who lived in a small, heated shack near the crematorium and who had "guidebooks" to sell, did we begin to understand what we were witnessing.

Majdanek had been designed to surpass Auschwitz in its size and efficiency as an extermination camp, but only a third of it was completed before the Russian army reclaimed southeastern Poland in 1944.[5] Still, its atrocities were no less horrible than those at Auschwitz or Triblinka; camp records tally over two hundred nationalities put to death there, including Americans. The majority,

[5] Lublin is less than 400 miles from the Ukraine border.

of course, were Poles. Other largely represented groups included Ukrainians, Hungarians, Slovaks, Romanians, Gypsies, and Jews. Several hundred Russian soldiers died at Majdanek, as did innumerable women and children.

The "flying saucer" monument, we discovered, was an arena-sized dome suspended above a pile of ashes and bones the size of an elementary school classroom. Nearby, and open to the public even on that drizzly Christmas Sunday, was the remaining crematorium. Upon entering it, we encountered breathless arrangements of bright, freshly cut flowers and 216 crosses, each one identifying (in several languages) its representative nationality.

We left shortly after that. Beyond the eerie emptiness of the place, and its flower-bedecked "ovens," Majdanek was not very informative as a museum, especially compared to Auschwitz. At the same time, there was something compelling about the place that made me promise to return another day.

The opportunity presented itself on a bright sunny afternoon in May. Andrew and I rode the bus to Majdanek. Having toured Auschwitz during our Fulbright orientation in Krakow back in September, Andrew had pestered me for months to take him to Majdanek so he could see the camp for himself.[6]

Despite the lovely early summer weather, Majdanek was nearly as deserted as when I had visited with the older children at Christmas. Andrew and I encountered only ten or twelve other visitors during our time walking around. We were, however, able to get inside the information

[6] Our two youngest, Andrew and Sarah, lived with me in Lublin. Sarah had no interest in visiting Majdanek, as "Auschwitz was bad enough." As it turned out, on that particular day Sarah was sunning on a beach in Spain. But that's another story.

center, as well as a few of the other buildings, where some displays remained. Other displays had been removed for refurbishing (we were told, though I wondered if that was merely the official explanation for the condition of the camp). It was obvious that funds were meager and community support poor. Majdanek was not included on Lublin tourist itineraries.

It was during my second visit, with Andrew, that I'd come to some understanding of why. They were *Ah-HA* moments, the kind writers—poets in particular—favor and hope to mine.

The first was at the information center. Built during the Soviet years, the building is a flat-roofed cement block structure of redundant single-paned windows, not unlike a rural 1950s school building. Paint on the outside of the building was flaking off in various shades of green or brown, like a sycamore tree, except for rectangular patches beneath some of the lettering, where perhaps someone had painted over Russian translations; the signs themselves were often missing letters, by the looks of them. The windows were hazy with age and airborne grime like many of Lublin's public buildings (at the time), as the infrastructure in Poland was badly in need of a little attention after forty-some years of Soviet-influenced neglect.

Inside was not much better: The walls needed repainting. Pamphlets and information brochures were negligible. The postcards were at least twenty years old. The condition of the place suggested to me that not only was there a lack of interest in maintaining a museum at Majdanek, but maybe it was even a kind of embarrassment to the residents of Lublin, a place they'd rather ignore.

What struck me second was in one of the barracks. It was filled with shoes—*800,000 shoes*, the sign said. Tossed haphazardly behind chicken-wire. Unlike Auschwitz, where mounds of suitcases and tons of human hair were carefully displayed behind neatly painted frames of glass, at Majdanek the exhibit was a sensory overload—warm, dark, and close. The bitter, acrid stench of tannin and sweat-soaked leather and human decay prevented us from staying very long.

The third was the sound of a warbler we heard as we escaped the barracks of shoes, stumbling, as it was, into sunlight. The song came from a field of grass where the prisoners once worked rows of cabbage, their primary food. I never saw the bird. But I heard the call distinctively, cheery and brilliant, in sharp contrast to what the museum stood for.

I admire the Polish people very much. They are friendly and considerate, even quite tolerant of well-meaning but patently-privileged American professors, despite their difficult history, rife with violent occupations, political partitions, cultural oppressions, and rogue ideologies. Yet their survival has meant complicity as well, even at the expense of human virtue. It has meant suppression and forgetfulness.

Our sadnesses may be chronic when the costs are high. And, to me, that's what Majdanek stands as a tribute to: the sadness of a life in which one is obliged to ride the bus to a death-camp each morning—delivering or preparing food, recording the dead, collecting belongings of those who perished—only to return by the same bus each evening to a cold, cramped apartment in the city. And being thankful for it.

THE POET AS IMMIGRANT:

NOTES ON "NEIGHBOURS"

Neighbours

ul. Langiewicza, Lublin

Every Sunday morning the hot water pipes
that run upstairs begin to whine
before buckling down and filling the tub above.

Water flows for quite some time—the pipes
narrow, galvanized, not likely up to code—
quiets for the length of prayer, then arias

explode as from a German-made hi-fi:
tenors booming tragically some swollen,
scratchy song. The recording's never something

I can recognize (although I grant my operatic
knowledge to be small). Other days I'm only
apt to hear her measured steps at meal times,

or a toddler's pitter-patter and ka-thunk
upon the unglued brown linoleum, an occasional
wooden wheeling of some child's riding toy.

I've seen them in the stairwell maybe twice.
She's thirty-something, I would guess—
a little pudgy, solemn, featureless. Both times

the child in her arms was so thickly swaddled
against the threat of cold
I couldn't tell if it was girl or boy.

N***eighbours***: The British (and consequently European) spelling of the title is intentional. The poem takes place in Poland, where I spent a year teaching American Literature and Culture as a Fulbright Scholar. Since my visiting professorship at Marie Curie-Skłodowska University (UMCS) was a full-time appointment, I was considered an immigrant and therefore had to register as such with the provincial government in Lublin. Beyond my students, who had acquired English either by attending secondary schools in England or Scotland (or, oddly, the Netherlands) or by having been taught by "foreign language" teachers trained in the Queen's grammar, very few Poles had more than a cursory understanding of English. But those who did, like the one or two residents of the apartment building where my children and I eventually lived, considered us *neighbours*.

Neighborhood connotes proximity, a geographically defined community, which some people acquire by choice, others by default. Neighborhoods are assumed to be internally dynamic. Whether or not one can be considered neighborly—that is, involves him/herself as a neighbor—depends in part on the nature of the individual, as well as the cultural nuances of the community. *Immigration*, in comparison, connotes a political separation—with status often determined by national boundaries and dictated by governmental policies (if not, in some instances, by ethnic or racial stereotyping and bigotry).

Neighbor is a term of inclusion; *immigrant* is a term of exclusion.

ul. Langiewicza: The epigraph to the poem refers to the address of the second of three apartments my children and I occupied during our year in Lublin. *Ulica* (abbreviated *ul.*) is the Polish word for street. We had managed only a few days in the first apartment assigned to us, which was university-owned and, by the administration's own admittance, "uninhabitable." Already scheduled for demolition, the grungy, one-room (and "sleeping area") apartment—which, we were told repeatedly, had served the prior (single) Fulbrighter more than adequately—was meant to be temporary, while renovations to the "new" faculty apartment were being completed. But "Poland being Poland"—as my department head explained—the projected completion date for the new digs had been pushed ahead, from "late August" (we arrived in September) to "maybe All Saints," to "the end of the year." Until then, the University had nothing else available, though if we were able to find more suitable housing on our own, the U.S.-Polish Fulbright Commission offered to help subsidize it.

The fact that we were Americans provided us with certain advantages while traveling through Europe—my colleagues at UMCS, a couple of whom had been to the U.S. as Fulbrighters themselves, referred to our passports as "golden"—but as immigrants, the search for long-term housing was a different story. Dorota, the young Polish woman assigned to us as a "shepherd" (that is, a translator and guide—a role tellingly defined today in the U.S. as "handler"), had a difficult time. Available housing in Lublin was rare and expensive. Most Polish families continued to share two- or three-room apartments clustered in massive, faceless Stalin-era housing developments—several generations together. (Living and sleeping rooms were indistinguishable in the room count; cooking areas and private baths were implicit, unless noted otherwise.)

A family was considered well-off if the grandparents had a room of their own, the children one of theirs, and the parents the luxury (and privacy) of transforming the main living area into a bedroom at night.

Most of the apartments Dorota was able to locate for us at an affordable cost were either too small or an untimely commute away from the university. Or the owner didn't allow children. In one instance, when Dorota initially talked to a woman about renting to "an American professor," the woman was all-enthused and invited us right over. The apartment was half of her lovely house—the whole upper floor—and she offered to do the cooking and cleaning for me in addition. I could even have a small dog, if I wanted one. But when she found out I expected to have my two children stay with me as well—without their mother—she rescinded the whole deal.

We found the second apartment, a two-room flat on Langiewicza, by word of mouth. It was convenient, at least, only two blocks from the university, and while in poor order, the owner assured Dorota over the phone that she was willing to make upgrades and repairs as necessary, if we signed a year's lease, at 800 zloty a month, two months in advance. If only because there was nothing else available, we agreed. But when we met to sign the lease—and our future landlady realized to whom she was renting (Dorota had learned not to say too much about us over the phone)—she claimed it had been a mistake. The lease was for 1,300 zloty a month.

Whether the cost changed because we were Americans or because we were immigrants, I can't say.

The definition of *immigrant* carries with it a certain stereotype—often a derogatory one. As does *American*, in many parts of the world. Yet Americans who have not traveled extensively beyond the politically defined borders of the United States never consider those parallels. Years of fostering our country's self-identification as global leader, a First-Class nation, superior in many ways to the rest of the world (in market, no less than military strength) have bestowed upon Americans a revisionist history, in which we ignore how much of the population of North America is, in point of fact, immigrant.

Hot water pipes: I'm embellishing here, as hot water for tubs and sinks was provided by individual wall-mounted gas-fired heating units, which, while noisy, made more the sound of a propane torch than clanking pipes. The hot water pipes that the apartments did have in common were those of the radiators, a pre-Stalin-era building-wide boiler system that, at best, provided us on the third floor with an average temperature of maybe 50 degrees.

Not likely up to code: The speaker, of course, is applying his own class and/or country's standards to a foreign situation.

German-made hi-fi: The prefix *im-* is shared by *immigrant* and *import*. In 1997, Poland was still much in the throes of Russian influence, as it had been since the end of WWII, not only politically but commercially and economically. German, in this case would have been *East* German, a country of enough economic reparation and cooperation with its western half to be able to manufacture limited electronics. *Hi-fi* is meant to suggest a certain lack of investment in modernization—my father had purchased his fabulous new RCA stereo hi-fi back in the 1950s—a detail not only meant to qualify the status of Polish infrastructure in general but to suggest a level of affluence nonetheless. The fact that the music is opera is telling.

It is also telling—I hope—that the speaker, who seems to cast aspersions about the neighbor because she apparently takes a bath and listens to music instead of attending church ("Ninety-five percent of Polish people claim to be Catholic," my department chair told me, "yet maybe four percent are *practicing* Catholics . . ."), is the same person who admits his own cultural narrow-mindedness, his unfamiliarity with opera.

Unglued brown linoleum: The unfamiliar makes us uncomfortable. Immigrants are, in some respects, unfamiliar. Neighbors, on the other hand, are manifest in similarities, if only by association. The speaker in this poem has not likely ever been in the apartment above his; he's only guessing as to what he hears, based upon the time of day, or maybe what aromas drift down. In describing the brown linoleum, he's projecting, given what he knows—that the apartments are all of a single design, of the same age, and that *his* kitchen has a shabby loose piece of brown linoleum covering what was probably the original well-worn gray-tiled floor.

Pudgy, solemn, featureless: What he does know, for sure, may be a kind of projection as well. The speaker doesn't get out much; he's an apartment dweller of the worse kind—not very neighborly, even as he implies that it's the unfriendliness of the woman from the apartment above that's the problem. Immigrant or not, he's as much of a recluse and stranger as she is. There is no eye contact in the stairwell. Perhaps he's as featureless to her as she is to him.

Thickly swaddled / against the threat of cold: "Cold" is meant to be ambiguous here. We don't know if the poet is speaking about the weather or about the Polish mother's tendency to thwart illness by preventing exposure to germs. And it doesn't matter really, because the point is the "threat," the danger of the unknown. That's what she is protecting her child from, which a perceptive reader would recognize as similar to the speaker's self-isolation, as evidenced by the details of his routine and domestic judgment, a metaphorical "swaddling," that is, of his own solitude and loneliness.

Couldn't tell if it was girl or boy: The fact that the speaker doesn't know the gender of his neighbor's child is not, as he is suggesting, the neighbor's doing. Rather, it's the speaker's. He has not made any more effort than she has. For that reason, the title is ironic. Neither the speaker nor his subject is very neighborly.

THE CURRENT U.S. POLITICAL and media attention to questions of citizens' rights and economic fairness tends to identify immigrants as *them*, neighbors as *us*. A practice—if not a policy—of exclusivity, to be sure. Not unlike the speaker of the poem "Neighbours," who, it seems to me, sets himself apart by setting himself apart, making judgments and assumptions about the people who live in the same building he does, neighbors by proximity—people he *assumes* are unlike him—instead of making the effort to be neighborly, to endorse our common humanity.

THE WRITER IN DRAG

Say I'm writing a fictional story that takes place in 1969. When the main character, Patsy, anticipates the arrival of the boy she's in love with, a boy she hasn't seen in nearly a year, I describe her feeling "both nervous and excited," and what immediately comes to mind about the ambivalence of her feeling, and how to describe it, is the scene from the movie *Armageddon* in which Oscar, played by Owen Wilson, is being strapped into the shuttle which will be launched into space on a mission to destroy an asteroid before it annihilates the Earth. When asked how he's doing, Oscar says he's got "that excited, scared feeling," which he then tries to articulate: "Like 98% excited, 2% scared . . . or maybe it's more . . . it could be 98% scared, 2% excited . . . but that's what makes it so intense . . . it's so confused . . ." Wilson provides a rambling, somewhat jittery description of what Oscar's feeling, which, I think, would capture Patsy's feelings perfectly, and I'm halfway through writing an allusion to the scene from *Armageddon* in an attempt to define Patsy's emotive state when it occurs to me that the movie wasn't released until 1998, thirty years after the purported time of Patsy's boyfriend's arrival.

The moment presents a dilemma. The feeling of nervousness and excitement, it seems to me, is the same between the two characters, and so the allusion to the scene in

Armageddon may help a film-nursed twenty-first-century reader to understand how Patsy felt in 1969, pumped and panicked at once. Since I am writing Patsy's story in the third-person point of view, it is entirely conceivable to have the narration make such a connection. It is, after all, fiction. And yet, as I am using the third person *limited* perspective—that is, writing from Patsy's viewpoint—I would be ignoring issues of character credibility by having her allude to moments that, in 1969, have yet to exist. Even if I reframe Oscar's "excited, scared feeling" in a perfectly plausible scenario, place it in a 1968-like film, or describe it in a trope of "as if," a modern reader might in recognizing the parallel also dismiss Patsy's moment as a knock-off.

I first saw *Armageddon* in 1999 or 2000 when I bought a used VHS edition on sale from Family Video. It is the same tape I reviewed just moments ago to make sure I was recalling Oscar's words accurately. I found it behind the DVDs in my TV cabinet. (Fortunately, I still have a VCR.) Who would have imagined in 1968 that such things as video cassette recorders and tapes would become (1) technologically possible, (2) affordable, (3) ubiquitous, (4) spawn a multibillion-dollar industry, and (5) become [nearly] obsolete in the wake of DVDs. Not Patsy. And that's not even considering the credibility of a *space shuttle*. In Patsy's day, Neil Armstrong has yet to walk on the moon.

Fiction, it seems, allows us to give our characters in the past a good deal of prescience, especially when it comes to things like human feelings, which I'm guessing have changed little over the millennia, and then mostly in terms of their articulation or interpretation, and less in their actuality. I'm guessing that basic human emotions haven't evolved in the way that technology has; I would like to think that we share the same feelings, or fears, or pleasures, or love, as people did in 1969, or 1669, or even 569 B.C. Don't we still read and perform Shakespeare or Aeschylus for the intensity of familiar emotion? And yet (some argue) the world is very different now, much more complex, and so the need to address human relationships within that complexity, to modernize them, has become more complicated because we now have more triggers, more exposure to sensory detail that would stimulate feelings, and so as a result we need to find new ways to evoke the human condition in terms of relativity! light years! deconstruction! quarks and black holes!

Not to mention smartphones and the Internet.

If nothing else, we certainly have more people in the world, more diversity, more complex individual choices, more opportunities for feelings. But does that make the feelings one person feels any different? Perhaps not. Though it does make our *description* of what we're feeling—or of what our characters are feeling—more difficult. Too common an allusion and we lose credibility to cliché; too far-fetched an allusion and we lose credibility to inauthenticity.

How little I knew in 1969! How often, at eighteen, was I confronted with feelings both exciting and scary, with confusion or ambivalence, similar to what Patsy feels as she anticipates the arrival of the boy she hasn't seen in a year, a boy she might be in love with, the boy who is *me* actually—highly fictionalized. I've written the story this way so *I* don't have to relive those feelings again, or try to describe them accurately, even if I could.

EPILOGUE: WHY I HAVEN'T WRITTEN MORE

Life without industry is guilt,
and industry without art is brutality.
— John Ruskin

Because I've been persistent enough to have published a little during the past five decades—poems mostly, but the occasional story and essay as well—I have acquired somewhat of a reputation in local venues as a "writer." Much of the reputation, I admit, is questionable, fostered in part by self-promotional author bios and/or public relations materials distributed through the organizations I've been associated with (not to mention the universities I've attended and taught at). Apparently, in the microcosm of rural, quasi-literary or academic communities, minor publications are worth heralding (most often as news fill during one or another local sport's off-season). As a result, acquaintances and colleagues are more likely to ask if I've been writing lately ("Working on something new?") than how my day is going or how my family is. I'm sure they mean well, given the televised stereotype of a writer's flamboyant ego and compulsion, but the persons asking such questions are often startled by my answer, which tends to cut short any subsequent niceties.

"No," I say. "Not really."

No false modesty is intended. Nor is my reply the consequence of curmudgeonly social graces (of which, occasionally, I've been guilty). Instead, it's simply the truth. I spend more time *not* writing than I do writing. Considerably more time. Over the past fifty years, in fact, I've developed quite a proficiency for not-writing. I've learned that not-writing is in many ways preferable to writing; not-writing makes a cheerful avocation.

I started not-writing in high school, shortly after I was "turned on" to contemporary poetry by Miss M., an enthusiastic (and very eye-catching) 22-year-old student teacher in my 11th grade American Literature class (which I'd been transferred into, mid-year, from an "equivalent" class taught by the retiring advisor to the school newspaper, who had us do little more than write news articles for the paper and who considered me—for refusing to do so—a "disruptive influence"). Come spring, under Miss M.'s inspiration (in more than literary ways, as "eye-catching" should suggest) and for lack of anything better to do during lunch period in the warm, blossoming quad of Traverse City High School, a couple friends and I began to compose something like poems. At first they were simply wild, rebellious, adolescent parodies of some Ferlinghetti or Cummings or Ginsberg poem we'd *had* to read in American Lit (if not pseudo-literary take-offs of something etched on the thickly-painted stalls in the boys' lav).[1] Yet the more we tried to embellish each other's outrageousness, the more clever and funny and entertaining our poems became (at least to us). I soon discovered a certain knack for composing such "poetry," given the laughter of my appreciative audience. I found a kind of pleasure in teasing meaning out of ambiguity: "I am a lamprey / I suck trout..." For the rest of the semester I played to an audience of hormonally-charged teenage boys, testosterone rising like sap. (Not to mention self-gratification.)

When summer arrived and we rising seniors took to seasonal occupations—cherry picking, life guarding, water skiing, beach bumming—I did too, to some extent. Yet unlike the others, who were anxious to leave behind any vestiges of schoolwork, I continued to jot down phrases and images all summer, just for the sake of doing so, filling one spiral notebook after another with musings and stories, which, as the weeks passed, moved beyond the crass, smart-alecky, hormonal ditties of Spring and toward what I was sure at the time were mature philosophical reflections on life, death, and unrequited love. Stirred by the aesthetics of my seventeenth summer—not to mention the idyllic sunsets, beaches, and bikini-clad tourists of the Grand Traverse region—I committed my senior year to a writer's life.

That fall I doubled up on English classes. At the time, high school seniors in Michigan working toward a College Preparatory diploma were required to take a fourth year of English and could choose either Composition or Literature. I signed up for both, thinking it would be good practice for a writing career. I wrote every chance I got. I feigned moodiness and preoccupation. While I didn't resort to wearing black turtlenecks and growing a goatee (which was genetically unlikely anyway), I was nevertheless convinced that I had been *chosen* to be a writer, and so I shared some of my work with my teachers—sophisticated, literate women who (I imagined) came and went from the faculty lounge talking of Michelangelo. I was sure they would be supportive. And despite their familiarity with my academic performance up until then, they were. Even to the point of assigning me two grades for work on which other students only got one, averaging a final score. I would get a *content* grade ("Original," "Creative," "Imaginative") and then a separate one for *execution* ("Learn to spell!"; "Review sentence structure!"; "PUNCTUATION!"). Not only was I bolstered to think that writing creatively could pay off so well—the content grade often outweighed the other—but my successes were surely evidence of a natural gift.[2]

Mrs. Stocking, my composition teacher, was particularly encouraging. She suggested that I submit a few samples of my work to the editors of *Challenger*, the TCHS annual literary and art magazine. Convinced that in passing along to them my three notebooks from the prior summer I would be enamored for my incredible gifts and promoted into the literary world with all the fanfare of a quirky baseball rookie, I did so. And was acknowledged accordingly. The editors selected three poems for duplication—more than any other student. At seventeen, I was about to become the next John Keats.

It was upon the distribution of *Challenger* that I first encountered not-writing. What I thought would be my launch into literary space was more like a flash fire on the pad. In print, the poems seemed different—*were* different, due to the number of typographical or editorial changes. When I confronted one of the friendlier editors and spoke vehemently of authorial intent, she replied that it really didn't matter anyway because *no one would know*—something I had never considered. Not only would very few readers recognize the changes, but hardly anyone (beyond the other writers and artists included in the *Challenger*) would even read the poems in the first place. Then, to add injury to insult, *someone* had apparently misplaced the three spiral notebooks I'd submitted—the only extant copies of what I had produced up to that time—which I had naively entrusted to the editors' care. I was never to get them back. Discouragement clung to me like a bad grade.

I didn't write for several weeks after that. Writing, it occurred to me, was too obviously a futile endeavor, especially since it involved editors, who, for the most part, were irresponsible (at worst) or inconsiderate (at best). *Thoughtless. Stupid. Self-centered. Narrow-minded.* I began to form a certain image in my mind of a typical editor—a heartless, insipid, insensitive being—and I assured myself that if I was ever to be asked for a poem or story again (—which I secretly hoped someone would someday do—), I'd proudly refuse. I'd let them beg.

"I'm not writing," I'd say.

I went off to college in Nebraska, as far away from Traverse City as I could, in the hopes of establishing myself on my own merits.[3] During my freshman year at Hastings, I wrote mostly on the sly, claimed "for my classes only," though was happy to share (and condemn) my copy of *Challenger*, whenever the question of "Poetry?" was raised. So when the announcement came soliciting material for *Spectrum*, the college literary magazine—a "real," professionally printed magazine (as opposed to the stapled mimeographs of *Challenger*)—painful memories of my high school experience left me less than enthusiastic. *I don't have time to write*—is what I told my literature professor when he encouraged me to submit. *My courses are very demanding.*

Which was not entirely true. Sure, I was not able to write creatively as often as I wished. But I *had* been writing, and so when I was badgered sufficiently (was, ahem, *begged*), I submitted an unruly folder of various things (under a number of pseudonyms) to one of the editors—an upper-class co-ed who'd impressed me as being open-minded (and who had once paid a good deal of [inebriated] attention to me at a party hosted by the English Department). Again, I was blessed with a couple acceptances.

On the day I received and read that issue of *Spectrum*, when I critically compared my freshman offerings to those of the more senior writers on campus, I decided I would never write—or at least never *publish*—again. I was embarrassed by my juvenilia.

It's been a life of not-writing ever since.

I don't write because writing is difficult—the most difficult thing I've ever done. It could be I'm too Type A when it comes to writing, but during those times when I can't help myself, I struggle so hard for *le mot juste* that the process often overwhelms the product. I tinker and fuss. I adjust. I re-adjust and re-tinker and fuss. The whole business is agonizing.[4] I type and retype for the sake of a comma or the choice of a word. I refuse to let my writing see light until I'm sure it's *exactly* the way it *must* be, which, when I return to it later, it seldom is. I'm seldom satisfied. (One reason, I suppose, why my first book did not appear until a month before my fiftieth birthday.)

I also don't write because it's not worth the effort. If the fees, prizes, or grants I've received for writing were ever calculated on an hourly scale, my desk would be in foreclosure. This realization was never so statistically clear to me as it was when a lucky grant in 1990 allowed me to purchase my first computer. Word Perfect tallied the number of minutes (and revisions) I'd taken to alter two words in a six-line poem. I was astonished—so much so that it soon became difficult for me to justify "wasting" any more time writing.

Writing takes a great deal of time, if those statistics are correct, and it's time I simply don't have (*he said*; see "How I Write Poetry," page 178). At least, not in large uninterrupted blocks, which I require; I don't write unless I can arrange massive amounts of available time. Yet, as someone once pointed out, "Time is a human measurement, and like everything human, we measure it according to its loss." Since massive amounts of available time happen once in a blue moon—and that's when I do my best work—I generally forgo writing. I refuse to start anything new.

How can *anyone* find time to write, what with all the daily demands of modern life? In college, of course, it's coursework. By the time I'd finished a Ph.D., I had amassed nine years of non-writing, including (ironically enough) three years of creative writing workshops at Bowling Green State University.[5] It's true I cranked out reams of weekly exercises, yet I never counted them as serious *writing*. (Nor did any of my peers, now that I think about it . . .). Instead, I considered those poems and stories to be mere practice—grade fodder—for the *real* writing I would do when I finished my degree and landed a cushy teaching position and so had time to show what I was capable of.

It never happened. While I consider myself fortunate to have been hired at Keuka College in a tenure-track position fresh out of grad school, I soon discovered that—time-wise—academe wasn't what I had expected. The pressures of accruing tenure and promotion, of designing and teaching composition and literature courses, of curriculum and instructional committee work, coupled with the time constraints of marriage—not to mention our wham-bang-boom method of family planning (three kids in five years, with a fourth three years later)—prevented me from writing.[6] The sustenance of my domestic life caused writing constipation.

That is, I don't write because I *teach* writing. Despite the carrot-dangling promises of holiday breaks and summers off, writing teachers are the true mules of academe. In addition to the preps and lectures, the intensive re-reading of critical and primary texts, the conferences with students, the curricular issues, the department meetings—there are knee-high stacks of essays or stories or poems to critique and grade. (And hardly enough daylight left to wash the car.) Besides, I'm wary of undue influences, of my own work either taking on the weaknesses of the horrible writing I'm wallowing in or of becoming mere imitations of the better examples. I simply can't create and critique at the same time. To write *well*, I believe, one must have distance from other people's writing.

Surely, if you've been reading this far, you're aware that over the years I achieved professional success as an academic: tenure, promotions, even an award or two for teaching. But it was not the cushy, graduate-level, endowed chair that I had envisioned. It was time-consuming work (no matter how economically supportive and professionally pleasurable it may have been). At some time during those years, my Muse—that ragged puppy—had turned away from whining at my door and had wandered off into the woods.

Frankly, I may be genetically predisposed to not writing. For that, I blame my mother, whose familial and domestic inclinations I've inherited (see "Stöllen," p. 83).

I've continually argued that "family comes first," that good employment, however demanding, is simply the foundation for the domestic pleasures one's family provides. I've also found that playing with my kids [and now grandkids]—visiting the zoo, digging in the sandbox, swinging, coloring, baking cookies, even shoe shopping at the mall—is a lot of fun, much more fun than writing. And isn't it healthy for children to spend quality time with their father? I essentially put my writing career on hold until our four children had grown up and moved on. Then, in my fifties, I became a househusband all over again, with a second family. Which not only took away any time I had to write but provided additional reasons for not-writing.

"It sounds to me like you're making excuses," a friend once said, "for nothing more than some kind of writer's block." A novelist and translator, whose regimen includes hours at her desk every day, whether or not she's productive, she invoked the words of a nineteenth century philosopher: "*Activity is not necessarily productivity. Even industry can be numbing, dull. We come alive when the dullness erupts.*"[7]

"Maybe your dullness isn't erupting," she said.

"Maybe not," I replied. "But it's got nothing to do with writer's block. If I have no time *to* write, where do you suppose I would find the time to *avoid* writing?"

I also don't write because I'm afraid of rejection. While over the years I have gotten better at discrediting those feelings of inadequacy that strangle me when an envelope

I've addressed to myself is returned in the mail [or, these days, I receive a form-reply email], nevertheless a short note telling me that there's no time (!) for a more personal catalog of my poem's weaknesses can still turn me away from the desk, send me out to weed the garden or mow the lawn. To do something more productive than writing. Rejection confirms one's inability to succeed as a writer. *Why bother?* I ask myself. And if it's not rejection *per se*, call it a lack of affirmation. *Close-but-no-cigar* is still a good enough reason to avoid making anything new. How many times must a writer be congratulated as a semi-finalist before he's convinced he's still a loser?

At the same time, I don't write because I'm leery of acceptance. When I survey the contemporary literary scene and find myself inundated with sham publications, the mediocrity of the po-biz, I don't write because I don't want to be included in that pool—to drown in the renaissance of the mundane.

Overall, in fact, in considering the contemporary literary scene, I'm not sure there's really a good reason for me *to* write. Not only do I have the "freedom" as an American to write about whatever I want (which, alas!, is not the same as the *will* to write), but I'm a straight, white, middle-class male from the Midwest, who grew up in a stable family environment. I have no ax to grind, no shame to confess, no cause to promote, no dysfunction to reveal, no guilt to redeem. Statistically, I'm a soccer dad (for nine years, a coach). I live in what could be called an up-scale neighborhood (though my house is one relic of pre-development). And I own two cars—one being a 1999 Mazda Miata, a [gasp!] sports car. I've been known to attend a Presbyterian church. Even my two divorces have merely whittled more notches in my demographic McGun. (Talk about no time to write! In the first instance, I became custodial parent of minor aged—then college attending—children; the second required the sale and purchase of two houses in two years—during the mortgage crisis—and a seventeen-year, Court-mandated co-parenting battle of a somewhat troubled [and totally troubling] child.)

All in all, I've had it pretty good—too good to have anything to write about. I don't write when I'm happy because the lure of sappy sentimentalism offends me, despite its obvious marketability (if the *Chicken Soup* series is any indication). And given the number of writers who *have* been abused, who have suffered through disturbing, unhappy existences—and by sheer will, persistence, or good luck been able to overcome the experience and write about it—that is, to be spokespersons for all of humanity—my experience falls short. If failure is one of the Grand Themes of literary art, I've failed at it. "*Real* literature gives immediate pleasure," says Maitland Boczek, one of my alter-egos, "but the sad fact of the matter is it's the *brevity* of pleasure which may simply account for the rest of one's miserable life . . ."

Which is not meant to suggest that I don't have things to write about. On the contrary, the things I *should* write about have prevented me from doing so (see the parenthetical about my divorces two paragraphs back). I don't write about love, for instance, because I've been beaten by it and I don't want to write any sniveling poems about divorce and loneliness—I see too many of those in the few periodicals I've found time to read. Nor do I write about the love I eventually fell into, the partner of my current daily pleasures. (I mean, who wants to read about *that* lucky stiff!) I don't write about death because more than once I have come too close—so close that it's still too painful to write about. (Or almost: see "Diving Lessons," p. 47). My parents are long dead; I spent the final couple years of their lives caring for them (and not-writing). They were kind, loving, generous, thoughtful people who, for the most part, lived quiet, comfortable lives. They loved their children unequivocally. There's no story there.

I also don't write because I have no self-discipline (as the perceptive reader has surely judged by now). I'm not willing to force myself to write. Long projects in particular frighten me; I'm afraid I'll never finish. I've yet to get beyond page 104 of the novel I began in 1973, for example. I'm more comfortable writing short, manageable things during short, manageable plots of time—those same hours that are better suited for other distractions, like biking, or baking, or *anything*, instead of writing. I don't want to get started on something and have to stop.

I don't write because I'm afraid that if I ever get started writing I won't be able to stop. The dullness will erupt, and I'll spend every spare minute of my life writing. I'll ignore my job, my friends, my social commitments. I'll abandon my children and grandchildren (and maybe end up in jail [or they will]); my dog will starve; my house will fall to ruins . . .

In the end, it's much easier *not* to write than to write, and the fact that not-writing is so easy may be the best reason of all for advocating it. Consider nine or ten years ago, when I first thought about starting this essay. For days I had to contend, instead, with ladybugs. The sheer number of *coccinella novemnotata* that collected in the unreachable corners of the kitchen and in the folds of the living room drapes—and that, in one instance, provided crunch to a pot of goulash—necessitated my direct, immediate action. I obviously couldn't write while ladybugs flicked against the window; I couldn't write while they flitted past my ear or snapped against the lampshade; I couldn't write while they massed along the ceiling. I knew they'd die in great clumps and likely get ground into the carpet and begin to stink. I was concerned that the dog would eat too many and become ill.

So I devoted my valuable writing time to vacuuming up ladybugs.

Oh, and then there are those endings. I've never been much good at endings. But as long as I'm not-writing, I won't have to worry about those . . .

Notes

[1] The loose-formed, colloquial poems of *A Coney Island of the Mind*—a paperback I may have "lifted" from Horizon Books (Mecca to a wannabe poet in Traverse City)—were especially archetypal. And one of Miss M.'s mimeographed handouts may have included Ferlinghetti's "Underwear," which would of course have prompted the theft.

[2] Only later did I come to realize that my small successes were more the result of grade inflation, sympathetic reaction to college student unrest, and—at least on the parts of some faculty—a seminal interest in post-modernism.

[3] Truth is, Hastings College was one of only two colleges I was accepted at, the other being Mackinac College, which, founded only three years prior, was yet to be

accredited. In its brief existence Mackinac was reputed to have the highest suicide rate (per capita) of any college. It was, after all, situated on an island in the Straits of Mackinaw, which could be inaccessible for weeks at a time if winter was severe. My decision was prescient, as the school closed a few years later.

4 Consider that I wrote everything in longhand at the time—to the consternation of my sociology professor—since I'd been bumped from typing class my senior year at Traverse City (waived from the State requirement) due to a shortage of typewriters. I had taken a typewriter to college—my mother's old portable Smith-Corona—on which I would type with two-fingers those papers that *had* to be typed. Mostly I used the machine to capture "finished" poems—which looked more finished in typeface—and which I would RE-type completely whenever I made a small change. To this day, I type painstakingly, with two or three fingers (not always the same ones), although it's on a computer now, a blessed invention for someone as revisionist as I am.

5 Not to mention that those of us lucky enough to have Teaching Fellowships also taught writing; we would be writing our own papers and grading student papers at the same time—time, to reiterate, we didn't have.

6 Much of which has already been described in other essays in this book, as the reader would know, if you'd been reading in the order they appear and not started at the back, as my wife tends to do.

7 I don't recall the name of the philosopher, or if she even gave one. I've never been able to locate the source. As she is a fiction writer, the words may have come from one of her own characters.

ACKNOWLEDGMENTS

Grateful acknowledgment is made to the editors of the publications in which versions of these essays first appeared:

Alimentum: "Stöllen"

The Broome Review: "Field Care of Game"

Detroit Free Press Magazine: "Robert" (as "Good-bye, My Brother")

Ferris Magazine [formerly *Crimson & Gold*]: "Occupational Hazards"

Fiction Southeast: "The Writer in Drag" (as "The Fiction of Credibility")

Fourth Genre: "Between Kennel and Creek," "Diving Lessons"

Immigration & Justice for Our Neighbors: "The Poet as Immigrant" (as "Immigration as a State of Mind")

Michigan Country Lines: "My Mother's Canoe Money"

Old Northwest Review: "A Lesson in Geography," "Once Bitten."

On-the-Town: "The Relish of Summer"

Pioneer [newspaper]: " Culture Choc," "Majdanek" (as two installments of "Up and Down the River")

POET: "Lost & Found"; "How I Write Poetry"

Referential: "Sandburg and Me"

TAB: A Journal of Poetry and Poetics: "Monkey Business"

Traverse Magazine: "Testing the Waters" (as "Morning at the Center of the Universe"); "Givin' Summer the Business"

Upstate New York: "The Perfect Tree" (as "Father Christmas")

Wake: Great Lakes Thought and Culture: "The Licorice of Politics"

"The Relish of Summer" won First Place for non-fiction in the adult division of the 2008 Grand Rapids Festival of the Arts Literary Competition. "The Perfect Tree" was twice reprinted as part of "Up and Down the River," a feature of the Mecosta County Humanities Council, in cooperation with *Pioneer* newspaper. "How I Write Poetry" has been reprinted in a number of publications, including *Pioneer* and *Ludington Daily News.*

"The Licorice of Politics," "Lost & Found," and "Diving Lessons" were each nominated for a Pushcart Prize.

With sincerest gratitude and admiration I'd like to thank Dr. Ross K. Tangegal and the extraordinary staff of Cornerstone Press (as noted on the copyright page), who have proved my early mental impression of editors in general to be grossly misrepresented. (Another lesson!) With diligence, care, and enthusiasm, they have given this book its life, and for that I am indebted.

Phillip Sterling is a poet and fiction writer. His books include *Mutual Shores* (2000), *In Which Brief Stories Are Told* (2011), *Amateur Husbandry* (2019), and *Local Congregation* (2023). He is the recipient of a National Endowment for the Arts Fellowship in Poetry, two Senior Fulbright Lectureships (Belgium and Poland), a PEN Syndicated Fiction Award, and artist residencies at Isle Royale National Park and Sleeping Bear Dunes National Lakeshore. He lives in Lowell, Michigan.

Milton Keynes UK
Ingram Content Group UK Ltd.
UKHW030103080824
446615UK00004B/263